Many Faces
of
Death and Grief

Many Faces of Death and Grief

DR. MARAL YERANOSSIAN

Liberty Hill Publishing

Liberty Hill Publishing
555 Winderley Pl, Suite 225
Maitland, FL 32751
407.339.4217
www.libertyhillpublishing.com

Many Faces of Death and Grief
First Addition

Paperback ISBN-13: 979-8-86851-603-0
eBook ISBN-13: 979-8-86851-604-7

For the remarkable individuals who have left this world yet imprinted their essence upon my life. Their legacies continue to inspire and uplift those who remain— especially my precious sister, Sonia Yeranossian, and my beautiful mother, Laurence Boyajian Yeranossian.

I will cherish your memory … until we meet again.

In Honor of My Greatest Teacher

*It is not the end of the physical body that should worry
us. Rather, our concern must be to live while we're alive—
to release our inner selves from the spiritual death that
comes with living behind a facade designed to conform
to external definitions of who and what we are.*

*The ultimate lesson is learning how to love
and be loved unconditionally.*

*It's only when we truly know and understand that we have
a limited time on earth—and that we have no way of
knowing when our time is up—that we will begin to live
each day to the fullest, as if it was the only one we had.*

—Dr. Elisabeth Kübler-Ross
(1926–2004)

Contents

Introduction

THIS BOOK HAS been taking shape my entire life. Since I was a young girl, I have witnessed death and observed people deal with it, fear it, and ignore it.

Thanatophobia is an intense fear of death or the process of dying. It is quite natural to fear death—an unexplained phenomenon—because we do not know when we will die or, most crucially, what happens when we do. Thanatophobia, however, is a clinical condition—an overwhelming anxiety about death and dying that can disrupt everyday life.

Everyone copes with death differently. Some turn to religion, others to science, and most try to ignore it entirely. They avoid conversations about the sick and dying as well as funerals and burials.

Grief is what follows death for those left behind and accompanies us through any ending that brings loss. It has been a part of me for so long that I wouldn't recognize myself without it—I depend on its quiet presence. I look for its phantom shadow to remind me not to rush into relationships. Grief holds my hand when I am apprehensive and sad. I want to share these experiences to reveal the benefits of recognizing your own loss and agony.

The first section of this book weaves together stories—some I have witnessed firsthand, others shared with me. If any resonate with you, I hope they help you find gratitude for your own journey—it's a part of who you are. The second section takes a broader look at grief: how people mourn, the influence of traditions and cultures, and the different ways we process loss.

One account tells of Arti, who, at the age of ninety-six, somehow died a perfect death—if such a thing is possible. She drifted away slowly, without pain, in the comfort of her home.

Three stories in this book are particularly personal to me. The first is about my sister's death at the age of twenty, a week before her college graduation in a tragic cold-case car accident. The second is about my mother's passing after enduring years of suffering, surrounded by loved ones in her home. The third is about my daughter's loss of hope in becoming a biological mother.

These narratives are filled with sadness but also hope. Grief is an emotion you feel because you have loved, cared, and lived deeply. It means you have built meaningful relationships, thrived in love, and experienced the richness of intimacy and the fulfillment of passion—some of the greatest gifts God can give us.

So, settle in and get comfortable—grab your favorite drink, wrap yourself in a soft blanket or cuddle up with a pet, and read at your own pace.

Wherever you are in your journey with grief, I hope these pages bring you solace, understanding, and a sense of connection.

PART ONE

Grief Narratives

Finding Peace

This story is presented from the perspective
of a relative who shared these events with me.

*People are like stained-glass windows. They
sparkle and shine when the sun is out, but
when the darkness sets in, their true beauty
is revealed only if there is a light from within.*

—Dr. Elisabeth Kübler-Ross

ARTI WAS ALWAYS a petite woman, barely five feet tall in her prime. At ninety-six, she seemed half that size. She had come from the old country where women were expected to obey and serve their husbands, bear many children, and devote themselves entirely to their families. Caring for herself was never an option—with five children to raise, she barely had time to brush her hair. Her husband, though soft-spoken, polite, and kind, was not a reliable provider.

Strong-willed and resilient, Arti did what her husband couldn't. A gifted seamstress, she supported a family of seven with her talents, knitting and stitching handmade outfits and tablecloths in a cramped two-bedroom apartment. Her firstborn, a daughter, was married off at sixteen to a much older man and moved away. Her second child, Seth, a boy, became a pillar of hope. More than a son, Seth was a friend and confidante, offering the support his father couldn't.

Arti relied on Seth for emotional and financial support where her husband fell short. She gave him the authority to manage the household finances, discipline his siblings, and make critical decisions for the family. She had high hopes for him. The remaining children—a second son, a second daughter, and the youngest son, Z—were expected to obey Seth and follow in his footsteps.

The family crossed continents, seeking a better life in the United States. In an unfamiliar world far removed from the one she was born into, Arti learned a new language, found work as a seamstress, lived with her husband,

and stayed close to Seth after he married. She played a key role in raising Seth's children, nurturing them with love.

When Seth launched a food truck business, Arti helped both financially and physically, waking up at 3:00 a.m. to cook. Her delicious food made it a success. After having three children, Seth's wife decided to join him in the business, taking over the cooking and leaving Arti to care for the grandchildren.

However, a rift developed between Seth, his wife, and Arti when the grandchildren started school. While she never complained or shared her problems with anyone, her younger children noticed the tension and urged Arti to move out. She finally did after her husband passed away—a decision that ultimately changed the course of her life.

For the fourth time in her life, Arti left the place she called home. After twenty-five years in the same neighborhood, she said goodbye to close friends and familiar surroundings to move into a modest apartment in a senior living community, closer to her daughter and youngest son in another city. Not long after she settled into her new environment, Arti lost her firstborn to cancer, leaving Arti with a broken heart and two vulnerable and grieving granddaughters.

Still, she adapted to her new life. She settled into the community, met her neighbors, made friends, and established a cozy routine and comfortable life. She often entertained and made her delicious and famous cookies for her visiting grandchildren. Yet, she yearned for the closeness of her beloved Seth and the grandchildren she had raised. They visited infrequently, and kept their distance, which tormented her and created conflict with the rest of her children.

By the time Arti turned eighty-five, her health had declined after several falls, each leaving her less mobile until she was confined to her home, relying on a walker and wheelchair. Her daughter suggested a nursing home. Arti reluctantly accepted the idea, until Z stepped in and vowed to care for her instead.

Married for nearly forty years with children of his own, Z moved in with Arti, ensuring comfort during her final years. He hired a caretaker to look after her while he worked, but was there, with her, every night and on weekends. He realized he had never truly spent time with her, *tête-à-tête*, never asking about her worries, her unfulfilled dreams, or her mistakes. He also confided in her about his struggles with Seth and how unfairly he had been treated by his older brother.

Z had many regrets, especially about decisions made for him, like sacrificing his love of art. His mother listened closely and nodded. They began to understand each other. Those days became precious to Z as he appreciated that she still saw him as the youngest child who had lived through the family's most difficult times, when their limited income had barely covered their basic needs.

Arti's nights grew restless with an overwhelming anxiety she didn't understand. She was scared and confused. Z would hold and soothe her until she slept. She often woke up soiled, unable to get out of bed. He would carry her to the bathroom and change her diaper.

Distraught and reluctant to accept her situation, she would say, "Oh, my son, I'm so sorry. This is not how I wanted to end up—shame on me."

"Don't worry," he'd reply lovingly. "Think of me as your daughter."

They'd laugh, but eventually, he stopped responding, too weary to ease her shame. There was nothing he could say to make her feel less embarrassed.

As the days passed, Arti grew weaker, speaking less and sleeping more. One rainy weekend, while watching a movie, she turned to Z and interrupted him while he was explaining the plot.

"Son, I wronged you. I gave the reins to the wrong son."

He was stunned. Tongue-tied, Z couldn't answer. Instead, he hugged her wordlessly as she fell asleep in his arms.

He carried her to bed. *The end is near*, he thought.

Arti slowly faded away through the summer months.

In mid-October, Z had a business meeting but decided, at the last minute, not to go. He headed home, grabbing takeout from Tommy's Burger—Arti's favorite fast food.

As he entered the apartment, Z heard her clear voice: "Son, is that you?"

"Yes, Mom, it's me. I decided to skip the meeting and picked up your favorite burger instead. Do you need anything?"

"No, God bless you, Son," she murmured.

He changed out of his work clothes, then started the kettle for their nightly tea when he sensed—rather than heard—a faint voice, a gentle nudge, urging him to check on her. Taking a deep breath, he knew. She was gone.

He stepped towards the bed and looked at his mother for the last time—sleeping deeply, forever at peace.

He kissed her hands and forehead, whispering, "I love you, Mom. Rest in peace."

Years later, Z explained that he had once been very angry at his mother for treating her five children so differently. His grief for her after she died was brief—he was no longer tormented or angry. He realized that he had begun grieving her long before she died. By the time he cared for her, she was no longer the mother he knew—she had become a child in need of help.

Still, he was thankful for their time together—and, that she had acknowledged his sacrifices.

"We talked it out," he'd say, reassuring himself. "And I have no regrets."

Guiding Light

This is a personal one—it was tough to write
but needed to be told.

*I didn't fully realize it at the time, but the
goal of my life was profoundly molded by
this experience—to help produce, in the next
generation, more Mother Teresas and less
Hitlers.*

—Dr. Elisabeth Kübler-Ross

MY MOTHER TOOK me into her home when everything I had built over twenty-five years fell apart. I was on the verge of bankruptcy, my family was torn apart, and I was despairing, in the pits of an abyss. My only light was my mother's faint voice, comforting me and asking me to move in to "take care of her"—a gesture meant to lift my spirits and make me feel better. But I knew the truth: she was once again carrying me in her old age.

At eighty-five, my mother was independent, diligent, faithful, honorable, and dependable. She still found ways to support the community, contributing sixty percent of her limited income to various charities. She loved to laugh, to praise God, and above all, she adored her daughters. She had already endured the unbearable—losing her firstborn in a tragic cold-case car accident at twenty. The grief had left her emotionally devastated until she found refuge in her faith, becoming a devoted Christian.

Our first year living together was bittersweet. Her poor health prevented her from driving, so I became her chauffeur. We spent a lot of time together. We laughed, cried, and indulged in chocolate cones from Baskin-Robbins, her favorite ice cream, which she loved so much. After every doctor's appointment, she devoured hers right there in the car, her childlike delight never fading. Sometimes, we'd treat ourselves to lunch after Bible study. We recorded prayers and filmed cooking videos, capturing fleeting, personal moments.

She gently touched my sadness with her beautiful words,

reminding me, in my hours of wistful stillness, of the two greatest blessings in my life: my daughters.

On our last Mother's Day together, my son-in-law found a kitten behind our shed and brought the animal inside. I expected my mother to reject it, just as she had with every stray that had entered our home since my childhood. Instead, she studied the tiny creature, then turned to me, and said, "This is yours. 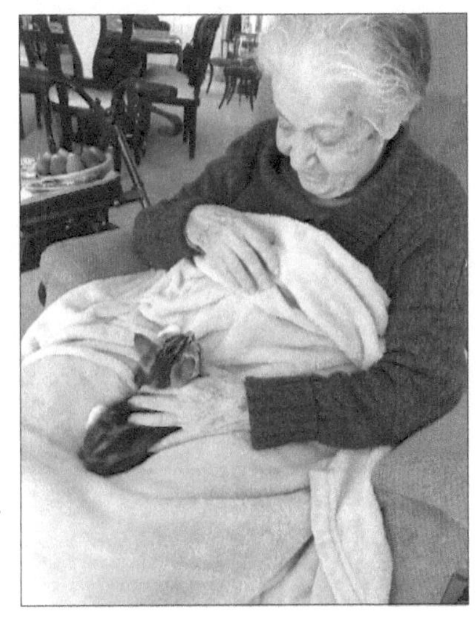 God sent it to you so you can take care of each other."

As Mom's health deteriorated, she formed an unexpected bond with the kitten, who we had named Bingley. He followed her everywhere, slept curled up on top of her chair, ran around her when visitors arrived, and even rode on her walker as she moved around the house. My mother was fascinated by the deep bond the cat formed with her and affectionately called him "her Dingaling."

When she lost another one of her brothers the following year, Mom handled it like a pro—with remarkable dignity and strength. She made sure that his family was never alone by offering constant emotional and spiritual support. That year, something shifted between us. My mother finally got to know me, and I, in turn, fell even more deeply in love with her spirit.

Then came the appointment that shocked us both, shattering our fragile peace. Her nephrologist confirmed what I had feared—having seen her test results: she was declining rapidly. Hearing it from the doctor made it real. Dialysis was an option, but not one he recommended. He told me there was nothing more he could do.

She looked at me and asked, "What is he saying?"

"I'll explain it when we get home," I murmured, reluctantly, though we both knew she understood. I resented the burden that fell upon me. *How could I tell her that the time had come?* I thought. *How do you tell your mother that the time has come to prepare for the end?*

On the drive home, I stopped at Baskin-Robbins out of habit.

"No, let's go home," she said.

"Just one cone. We can share if you want," I urged. She relented, but when I handed her the ice cream, I heard her ask, "How long do I have?"

"You know very well that the doctors don't know. Fifteen years ago, you thought you only had five years. Who knows? With your prayers, you might live another fifteen years," I said, trying to sound cheerful.

She ate her ice cream, but, for the first time, handed it back to me after just two bites.

"I don't feel like it," she said.

Her voice was soft, the fight gone. The defeat in her spirit left me heartsick.

Her health quickly deteriorated four months before her passing. She was in and out of the hospital until her HMO, at her last discharge, asked us to consider hospice. Mom gazed at me, terrified, thinking I would place her in a home.

"Are you going to put me in a home? I want to stay at my house, please …"

"I would never do that, Mom. You'll always wake up in your home, in your own bed, with your beautiful garden just outside."

A compassionate nurse gave me the brochures for in-home hospice, and I signed the papers, announcing that I would take care of her.

The Final Weeks

*Watching a peaceful death of a human being
reminds us of a falling star; one of a million
lights in a vast sky that flares up for a brief
moment only to disappear into the endless
night forever.*

—Dr. Elisabeth Kübler-Ross

WHEN THEY HEARD the news, her daughters and grand-daughters gathered around Mom. Somehow, she seemed more aware that something was happening—perhaps because visits like these were rare. She looked at everyone wistfully, grateful for the company, knowing that tomorrow might not come.

In the weeks that followed, my mother's behavior changed drastically. She became moody and agitated about everything. But her disposition was the least of our concerns—her body was shutting down, one organ at a time. Walking became difficult, and eating, except for sweets, was nearly impossible. She could no longer make it to the bathroom on her own. Nurses and phlebotomists visited daily.

Her agitation turned on me. I became anxious, exhausted, and constantly on edge. She was like a frightened little girl—angry at the world and at me, yet powerless to do anything about it.

One afternoon, I found her lying down, staring at nothing.

"Let me see your hands," she said suddenly, her voice urgent.

I extended my hand, but she grasped my entire arm.

"You have my arms and hands," she whispered, her eyes welling with tears.

"Mom, are you scared?" I asked.

"Why would I be scared? I have Jesus, and I know where I'm going," she reassured me. "It's just … it's so hard leaving you all. I will miss you."

I caressed her head, ran my fingers through her hair, and held her as she fell asleep in my arms. I cried silently.

Week One

I WOKE UP, jumped off the couch, and ran to Mom's room. She had been calling me.

"I'm sorry I'm waking you up every night," she said. "I don't trust myself to get up."

"Don't worry, Mom. You know I don't sleep much."

The evenings were the worst. A proud and dignified woman, she refused to soil the adult diaper she'd been wearing. She wouldn't let her daughters clean up after her, knowing what it meant.

By then, her kidneys had stopped functioning. Her feet were swollen and leaking fluid. The doctor said she would not last long.

Just days before Christmas, the hospice physician called to tell me that Mom wouldn't make it to the holidays. I had planned to have the whole family over so she could see everyone one last time.

One of the hardest things I did was maintain the charade: "No, Mom, I just want to have Christmas here since you couldn't go to the party at our cousin's house last year. You'll be fine, Mom."

She looked at me—the sharp, astute woman who always read my looks and reactions—and shook her head.

On Christmas Day, her brothers and their families

gathered at her house, but she refused to get out of bed. I understood. She was delaying the inevitable. She knew that if she got up and faced her family, it would be for the last time.

I shamelessly threatened her.

"Listen to me, Mom. If you don't get up right now, I will tell them all to leave."

I must have been convincing because she slowly sat up and walked into the living room, where everyone greeted her with smiles and kisses. I watched her trying to seem relaxed, trying to seem happy. She didn't look at me again that night. She barely ate and excused herself to go back to bed. But not before she blessed us all with a prayer.

Weeks Two and Three

EACH MORNING, MOM got up diligently from her bed. After I washed and dressed her, she would come out, greeting everyone and attempting small talk—only to drift off to sleep on someone's shoulder.

Each evening, she sat at the edge of her bed, offering a tender prayer for us. I would change the soaked pad, clean her legs, and say, "Let's do it the same way: cross your arms and let me turn you as you lie down."

She did as I instructed, but each time, a painful cry escaped her lips.

"I'm sorry, Mom. Did I hurt you?"

"No, no. It's not you—it's never you."

This routine repeated itself a few times a night. Mercifully, she returned to sleep quickly and wasn't in pain for long. I would go back to the couch, turn on the baby monitor and listen for any sounds from her, and watch the sunrise.

The mornings brought calm and quiet, giving me hope. But I also knew her days were numbered. I felt her pain.

Week Four

MOM WOKE UP and barely made it to the living room. She didn't stay awake. She barely ate. She couldn't lie on her back—it made breathing impossible.

The doctor had told me she was drowning from the inside. The thought terrified me. I prayed, guilt-ridden, for God to make it quick.

We tried to involve her in conversations, but she only responded to prayers and Bible readings. Her breathing was so labored that we kept the ventilator on permanently.

The hospital bed we'd been waiting for finally arrived. She could now sleep comfortably propped upright. The hospice nurse started her on a morphine drip every two hours. Before leaving, she pulled me aside and said, "For all of your sakes, I hope she passes tonight."

Mom woke up within the hour and started having seizures. Her speech was incoherent, but she looked directly at me and reminded me not to forget to send in her donations. She recited *Psalm 23* along with us, then closed her eyes.

Another nurse who was in the room, seeing my horrified face, asked me if I wanted him to stay with us. I hesitated, confused, but then I realized: he was anticipating her passing. I nodded.

We all fell asleep on the couches around her bed. The nurse administered one last dose of morphine. And, while we slept, Mom slipped away and out of our lives forever.

❧

I had been preparing for this moment for months. But no amount of training in psychology, hypnotherapy, and meditation could have prepared me for the reality of it.

I tried to hold on, to be brave, telling myself she was in a better place, only to fall apart, again and again.

My mother was a vibrant, opinionated, and sassy woman. She was deeply devoted to God and the most silent feminist I had ever known. She made sure we worked hard and went to college because she never had the chance. She sat with us night after night while we studied, making sandwiches, coffee, or tea. She lived vicariously through our triumphs and wept for our sorrows.

She was also a quiet warrior. She fought for the underdog. She defended the weak. She was passionate about her beliefs but open-minded to different points of view.

She left me her house because I had lost mine. After the funeral, when I returned home—*her home*—I felt homesick.

Because my mother was my home. And she wasn't there anymore.

Her passing left a hole in my heart and pain in my soul.

The End of an Era

DECEMBER 30, 2018, marked the end of an era. For a long time after her death, I would wake up in the middle of the night and race into her bedroom, convinced I had heard her calling—only to find an empty bed. Bingley mourned too, spending his days in her room, seeking comfort on Mom's pillow. But I could neither sleep in her bed nor next to the cat for consolation.

Sometimes, when I cooked Mom's culinary specialties, I would feel a breeze when there was no wind, and that convinced me she was watching over me. I promised to keep my mother's spirit alive in her house. She loved new things—furniture, clothes—so I started renovating her home. I bought furniture she had once admired, remodeled her kitchen, and revamped her yard. I thought all these tiny improvements would make her happy when she looked down on us.

As a culture, Armenians remember the dead annually on the day of their passing. My mother lost her eldest daughter, my sister, on her own birthday, so she stopped celebrating it. Now that she was reunited with her child, I decided to celebrate her birthday again—with a party, inviting all her family. For her special day, I cooked the foods she loved and welcomed her brothers and their families into her home.

Two days before the party, my mother came to me in a dream. She walked around the gathering, admiring the decorations and the food. With a pleased, almost child-like voice, she told me, "Oh, my, you even got candies I love and *lahanayov sarma*!" The cabbage-wrapped dish—an Armenian favorite—was one I had not made without her.

I woke up startled because I wasn't planning to serve candies or that particular dish. So, I immediately went to work, ordering the candies and preparing the food she had mentioned. I believe, in her own way, she was letting me know she was happy about my decision to celebrate her birthday—and that was more than I could have asked for.

I can't conclude this story though without mentioning Bingley—the cat my mother took in for me, who ultimately became hers. In the months after her passing, Bingley fell into deep mourning. He had been with her throughout our time together. When mourners came to the house, he retreated to her bedroom, curling up on the tiny seat of her walker. He stayed there, refusing to eat or drink, through the visitors' comings and goings.

When the house finally quieted down after everyone left, he searched for her. He lingered in her room, waiting for her to return.

Bingley had always been a vocal cat, known for opening doors and calling out to us, as if by name. After Mom passed, I didn't hear a peep from him. He spent his days sleeping in her closet, on her clothes.

After I packed up her belongings and sent them to Armenia as donations, all that remained was her bedding, which I stacked on the highest shelf in the closet to deal with later. After all the sorting and packing, Bingley vanished. It took me two days to find him—nestled in her bedding, hidden away on the top shelf. No amount of treats or coaxing could bring him back down for three days.

My mother has been gone for five years now. Yet even today, when Bingley gets upset, he hides—and his safe place seems to be with her, in her room. I never knew a cat could mourn so profoundly. Now, I cherish my days with Bingley. We take care of each other, and together, we mourn my beautiful mother.

Enduring Spirits

This story is presented from the perspective of a relative who witnessed the events.

Those who have the strength and the love to sit with a dying patient in the silence that goes beyond words will know that this moment is neither frightening nor painful, but a peaceful cessation of the functioning of the body.

—Dr. Elisabeth Kübler-Ross,
On Death and Dying

THEIR LOVE STORY was effortless: two new immigrants in a foreign country, searching for a partner to build a life with, found each other. He was handsome, polite, soft-spoken, and kind, but had little financial wealth. She was beautiful, bold, full of life, and eager to embrace this new chapter together.

They married, made a home, and raised three children over forty-four years, even enduring the tragic loss of their eldest at a young age. He faced several challenges, including depression and job loss, while she, determined to support their family, returned to school, earned her credentials, and secured a respected position nearby. In time, he found steady work again, and they began to travel the world, savoring each other's company.

Their life became stable, even happy—until an unknown fever landed him in the hospital for months. As she cared for him, she dismissed her own persistent bleeding as stress, vowing to seek medical attention once he recovered.

Her first visit to the doctor was confusing. She struggled to understand his words. When he recommended surgery, she went along with it, unquestioning. No one knew exactly what the procedure was, but they didn't ask—culturally, they were taught that doctors know best. Who were they to question him?

Until she was finally diagnosed with cancer.

She endured treatment after treatment, each one proving to be in vain. The last treatment left her permanently in the hospital, unable to move.

To friends and family, she often shared, "I am so tired, I'm done, ready to go." The words were both resentful and wistful, heavy with pain and exhaustion.

He stayed with her, coming home late each night, weary and drained. His strength and stamina were buried under a sea of worries.

Was she going to get better? How will I live without her? I don't know how to live without her … Then, almost defiantly, he'd reassure himself: *No, no—God will make it better. God won't let her die. This is our time. We worked hard all our lives for this—to finally be free, to finally enjoy each other.*

Last Day

HE COLLAPSED ONTO the couch, his body sinking into exhaustion. Minutes later, he opened his eyes, disoriented.

Slowly, he sat up and looked around, grounding himself. The clock read 3:00 p.m., but his mind failed to process the time—or the fact that he had been asleep for twelve hours.

He whispered a prayer, reaffirming his faith: *Today will be a good day. The doctor will have good news for him. The chemo will have worked. She'll be coming home soon.*

With renewed hope, he stepped into the shower, letting the water wash away his worries, placing them in God's hands. He got dressed and reached for the cologne she loved. He scanned the house, making sure everything was in order—just in case they brought her home. Everything looked fine. Then, the phone rang.

"Where are you, Dad? Mom is asking for you," his son's voice came through.

"I'm on my way. Did the doctor come?"

"Not yet. Hurry."

A flicker of optimism rose in him: the doctor usually delivered updates early, but he hadn't come yet.

That must be good news, he told himself. *God is answering my prayers.*

When he arrived at the hospital, her room was filled with relatives. They greeted him with silent nods and gentle pats on the back, their words a blur.

She was awake, her eyes scanning the room until they found him.

"Where have you been? Everyone is waiting for you. I can't believe you weren't here."

Leaning in, he kissed her forehead.

She wrinkled her nose. "What's that smell?" Squinting, she realized what it was. "Oh, you're wearing cologne. How nice. I'm suffering here, and you're pampering yourself," she said bitterly.

He smiled. "But this is the one you got for me. I wore it for you."

"I don't need your cologne," she muttered. "I want to go home. I miss my home. I love it. Please, take me home."

Before he could answer her, the sedatives pulled her

under again. He adjusted her pillows and gazed down at her. The woman who once radiated strength now lay frail before him. Her thick, beautiful hair was gone, her face and body were swollen. And while she was fragile now, she was heavy, making it tough to move her.

A voice broke through his thoughts: "Why can't we take her home? She wants to go home."

He looked up, dazed and confused, at the cousin who had spoken. His mind refused to absorb any more information. After a long pause, he replied, "The doctor didn't advise moving her."

And then, suddenly, it hit him: *this is it.*

The doctor hadn't suggested moving her because there was no point. He didn't check on her as often because there was nothing more to be done. She was taking morphine every two hours. Her body was swelling. Her eyes were glassy.

He pressed his forehead into his palm. "God … this is it?"

Tears blurred his vision as he paced the room, adjusting chairs, tossing out paper cups, mumbling incoherently, nodding when asked a question—any small act to keep himself from unraveling.

She stirred again and opened her eyes. Her friend was by her side, gently caressing her forehead.

"Hey, why don't I put some lipstick on you? Maybe a little perfume?"

A faint smile played on her lips. "Why not?"

Amid the dense aura of the crowded room, the friend

dabbed lipstick onto her lips, spritzed her with perfume, and adjusted her blankets.

She scanned the room until she spotted him, standing frozen in the corner. With effort, she reached out a trembling arm toward him. He rushed to her bedside, took her hand, and kissed it. Slowly, she slipped off her wedding ring and placed it in his palm. He kissed the rings, then her shivering lips, his heart breaking with every movement.

She drifted off under the morphine's pull again.

Around him, the relatives whispered, looking at them with sympathy. The room buzzed with fragmented conversations—about the hospital, the food, the room. Their voices were muffled, their words meaningless.

Finally, the doctor walked in. His voice was gentle but firm. "I'm so sorry. We tried everything, but she's not responding. It's time to say your goodbyes."

A pause. "How long?" someone asked.

A sigh. "We don't know exactly, but … I don't think she'll see the sunrise."

An hour later, she opened her eyes once more. Her sons stood around her. She smiled weakly and murmured to them, "I love you."

Again, she searched the room for him. He stood behind the door, trying to hold back tears. *She wouldn't want to see him cry,* he thought. She hated that.

But she could feel him. "Aha," she said, in a waning voice. "You're here."

He stepped forward. "Of course, I am. Where else would I be? Remember what the priest said? We are one. We will never be apart."

She smiled and, in a faint voice, said, "Till we meet again."

Then, she closed her eyes.

And took her last breath.

He kissed her for the last time and, with words full of sorrow, he said, "Till we meet again, my love."

Comforting Souls

A mother narrates two stories from her perspective. While her children are mentioned, they were not involved in the storytelling.

For those who seek to understand it, death is a highly creative force. The highest spiritual values of life can originate from the thought and study of death.

—Dr. Elisabeth Kübler-Ross

Troubled Tigi

TIGI JOINED OUR family to take the place of Romeo, my children's first cat. Romeo, a Siamese mix with exquisite aquamarine eyes, had been given to us by my sister-in-law, who had found a litter of kittens underneath her house. Raised to believe that animals should live outdoors, I insisted he stay outside with our dog, Cello. They became close friends, playing, eating, and sleeping together. Though Romeo often wandered into the neighbors' homes, he always found his way back. I didn't realize how much comfort and joy these animals would bring me in the years ahead.

Selling our house to improve our circumstances, unknowingly set the stage for heartbreak. Catching Romeo and bringing him to our new home five miles away was no easy feat. Unfamiliar with transitioning a cat into a new environment, we placed him in the backyard—he soon escaped. Romeo fled one day and vanished. Lauren, my baby girl, was devasted. Her sorrow broke my heart. Night after night, I heard muffled sobs and whispered prayers.

"God, please bring Romeo back to me. I promise to take better care of him, love him more, and keep him safe. Please, God, I will do whatever you want—whatever Mom wants. Just bring him back."

A week of her pleas broke me. I couldn't bear her cries any longer. Desperate to ease her pain, I got her a tabby kitten with tiger stripes. Lauren hugged her and named her Tigi.

Watching my daughter's eyes fill up with tears as she begged to keep her new companion in her room, I couldn't say no. Tigi stayed with Lauren, and they became inseparable.

Tigi was every bit the playful, affectionate, and mischievous kitten. She leapt about, broke china, climbed into closets, shredded clothing, and chewed on anything she found. Everyone was exasperated except Lauren, who cradled her like a baby, adorning her with ribbons and hairpins.

One day, while the house was empty, Tigi sneaked into my older daughter Dawn's room. She rummaged through her makeup, smearing herself with lipstick. She knocked over perfume bottles, breaking them. Amidst the destruction, she curled up in Dawn's bed, grooming herself. That was how Dawn found her and the scream that followed when the mess was discovered was likely heard in the next town. She swore she'd kick Tigi out!

Lauren, ever the peacemaker, pleaded, "Please don't. I'll clean your room every day. I promise! I'll give you all my Christmas money, so you can replace what she broke."

As the years passed, life took unpredictable turns. We moved to a larger, two-story house, but Tigi never quite settled in. Lauren, now a teenager, had other interests, and the cat, sensing the shift, acted out—peeing on her belongings in protest. This led to her banishment from Lauren's bedroom. With nowhere else to go, she wandered through the vast house in search of refuge, eventually taking over Dawn's bedroom, which had been vacant since she'd moved out to be closer to work. Tigi wasted no time marking her scent everywhere.

A year later, two rescue puppies entered our lives, turning Tigi's world upside down. While the dogs were a blessing to us, they soon became Tigi's worst nightmare. Their rivalry became permanent; Tigi was confined upstairs, leaving the dogs downstairs.

Then, the wheel of life took another turn for the worse and our family had to move again. My husband left to care for his terminally ill mother. To minimize stress, we separated the pets. Tigi went with him, while the dogs stayed with me in a small studio guesthouse. In her now-quiet space, Tigi thrived. She bonded with my ailing mother-in-law, offering warmth and affection in her final days. When she passed, Tigi made one last move—to live with Dawn.

By then, Tigi was eighteen. Frail but content with her new life, she spent her days perched on Dawn's desk, watching her work and eyeing the birds outside. Dawn enjoyed her company: Tigi was a quiet, gentle companion and an excellent listener.

But time is merciless. Tigi's health soon deteriorated. She grew thin, confused, and incontinent. Her vision faded, and she barely ate. The vet attributed it to old age. During the COVID lockdown, we waited for her to slip away naturally. When her suffering became undeniable, Dawn made the painful call to a visiting vet.

I had always been told, "It's just an animal," that their suffering could never compare to human pain. As I looked at Tigi, I knew how wrong that belief had been. She had been frustrating yet endearing, her bright eyes and soft fur capable of changing our moods from sadness to joy. Her quirky behaviors had molded our lives in ways I never expected. And now, we were asking someone to end her life. The anguish of having to make that decision will never leave me: taking a life to save it from suffering.

When the vet arrived, my husband held Tigi close as she was being examined. She flinched at the stranger's touch, instinctively sensing something was wrong. Did she know? She was blind and couldn't see who touched her. Was she scared? My husband drew her closer. In his arms, she was just a little ball of fur, her head tucked into his elbow. I, too, wanted to comfort her but didn't know how—she had never really warmed up to me over the years, so, I kept my distance. Dawn, inconsolable, questioned if she was making the right choice.

The vet told us to say our goodbyes. She assured us that it would be quick but didn't say if it would hurt. As she administered the injection, Tigi let out a sharp, loud cry, her eyes flying open. She stared at us. Was she blaming us? Or was she simply saying goodbye? We will never know. A breath later, she was gone—asleep in infinity.

Gazing at her still, lifeless body, I whispered, "I'm sorry, Tigi. I'm sorry I wasn't a better parent. I'm sorry you were moved from place to place. And most of all, I'm sorry that we had to do this to you."

Those amber eyes will forever haunt me—questioning. The inadequacy I felt in caring for that innocent being weighed on me.

Lauren, unable to be there due to COVID restrictions, stayed silent, her swollen eyes speaking for her as we delivered the news on FaceTime.

"I wish I'd been there to say goodbye," she said quietly.

After the pandemic, Dawn moved back to her apartment but refused to adopt another pet—Tigi's loss was too deep. Lauren, the eternal animal advocate, continues to rescue, foster, and adopt strays. Though she'll never forget Romeo or Tigi, she ensures every animal in her life receives the love and care she once wished she could have given them.

Louie a.k.a. Louigi Bocharini

SEARCHING FOR DOGS became my mission as my daughters prepared to leave home—Dawn for work fifty miles away, Lauren for university. Was my longing for dogs a subconscious cry to keep them home, or a fear of them facing life alone?

Dawn had her heart set on a purebred Shiba Inu, complicating my search. Eventually, I found a foster parent with a pregnant Shiba Inu who birthed two puppies—part Chihuahua, part Pomeranian. Louie resembled his mother; Harvey, the fluffier one, looked Pomeranian.

Their foster mom, a handbag enthusiast, had named them after famous designers.

Surprisingly, Dawn bonded with Harvey and not the Shiba Inu, while Lauren fell in love with Louie. When Dawn moved into her new place, Harvey struggled. Both had a hard time adjusting to the new situation. Still a puppy, Harvey couldn't handle change and began having seizures and throwing tantrums, which forced him back to our home.

Meanwhile, Louie proved to be exceptionally intelligent, quick to learn, and deeply affectionate, particularly toward Lauren. His intuition was remarkable; he could sense when Harvey was about to have a seizure and would warn us. He became Harvey's protector, a big brother in every sense.

Like all puppies, both were rambunctious, loving, and happy. Though we'd moved into a bigger house, we struggled financially. When Lauren moved on campus and into a dorm, she couldn't bring Louie along. Working from home, I welcomed the company, even though I had little experience caring for animals, let alone two energetic puppies.

I attempted to apply what I knew about Pavlovian training, but Harvey's condition made his concentration erratic, leaving his brother to entertain himself. Louie loved to explore and enjoyed the outdoors. He also became protective of us—much like a guard dog.

Eventually, we moved to a smaller place with a large backyard, which delighted the dogs. They rolled in the grass, destroyed the rose bushes, and chased squirrels into the fruit trees. I had never seen Louie happier. I also realized that having too many "masters," had rendered any previous attempts to train the dogs futile. Harvey's excessive barking upset the neighbors, and we were advised to "take care of the problem." Someone suggested a shock collar, but we quickly dismissed that option as inhumane.

Louie, on the other hand, was a deeply compassionate dog. Through many of life's ups and downs, I would retreat to a secluded place to cry. No matter where I went, Louie always found me and sat beside me, resting his head on my arm.

I wasn't sure why he always comforted me. I wasn't the one fawning over him, nor was I playing with him or taking him on walks. Occasionally, I would feed him treats and clean up the messes he made. Over time, I noticed he did the same for everyone. He was a godsend. In his silent, gentle way, he held our family together, reassuring us that everything would be fine.

The following year brought major changes to our family. Lauren got married and moved out, taking Louie and Harvey with her. My daily life felt empty without my four-legged companions, but they thrived in their new home, enjoying their own space and a yard to run in.

After his tenth birthday, Louie began losing teeth, one by one, until he was left with none. Despite this, his energy never waned; he still chased balls at every chance he got.

Slowly, over time, his breathing grew heavy, and he started wheezing, barely able to catch his breath. The vet diagnosed him with pneumonia and prescribed medication, which only provided temporary relief. The pneumonia returned with a vengeance. Eventually, unable to keep down food, he grew sluggish and frail.

Desperate to nourish him, Lauren and her husband Noah would hold him upright, feed him tiny pieces of food, and massage him afterward. Their efforts helped for a time, but his breathing worsened. After a prolonged battle, the vet recommended putting him out of his misery. One Saturday, I received a call from Lauren.

"Mom, we're taking Louie. It's time."

"Tell me where—we'll be there," I replied, trying to sound calm.

My husband and I rushed to the pet hospital with Dawn, where we found Lauren and Noah holding each other in an embrace.

"Has it happened already?" I asked.

"No, they're examining him first."

We sat in the waiting room, surrounded by cheerful pet owners and glossy ads for premium pet food. Having recently lost my mother and a beloved cat, I wondered if I would ever grow accustomed to grief—if it would ever get easier. Would a time come when death became a norm, when the hurt dulled enough for me to catch my breath? Looking at my daughters and son-in-law, I felt heartache knowing that they, too, would face many similar moments of sadness throughout their lifetimes.

Finally, we were called into the "family room," where they brought Louie in. He was weak, but calm. He nuzzled his mom, Lauren, and scanned the room as if to ask why we were all there. Noah sobbed quietly in the corner, where Dawn handed him a tissue. My husband, who had given Louie's full name—his sobriquet, *Louigi Bocharini,* after the composer—struggled to keep his composure.

With the quiet strength of a tree, Lauren held Louie close and whispered, "I love you, my boy. Thank you for giving me so much happiness, for loving me, for taking care of me, and for being mine."

Louie rested his head on her chest, a picture of pure tenderness and love. He breathed in her scent before lifting his head and turning to my husband, who embraced and kissed him, whispering loving words through his tears. Then Louie looked around again, signaling that he wanted to go down. Though barely able to walk, he made his way toward me. With great effort, he lifted his head, meeting my gaze with his beautiful, but tired golden amber eyes.

I caressed his ears as I always had, held his face in my hands, and kissed his forehead.

"You are my angel, and I will miss you forever," I said.

Louie moved toward Dawn, who had knelt on the floor, hugging him in silent grief. At last, he stopped at Noah, who carried him back to Lauren. Together, they held him as the vet entered the room, needles in hand.

"It won't hurt," she assured us before administering the injection. Louie's eyes slowly closed as Lauren whispered, "You did good, my boy. Rest in peace, my love."

Both Lauren and Noah adore animals. They often cry and remember Louie, but their grief never stops them from fostering and adopting strays or helping any animal in need. They channel their loss into a positive outlook, grateful for the opportunity to have known and loved their animals. They have transformed their sorrow into a shrine for those they've lost, ensuring their memory endures throughout their lives.

Soulful Passage

Learn to get in touch with the silence within yourself and know that everything in this life has a purpose, there are no mistakes, no coincidences, all events are blessings given to us to learn from.

—Dr. Elisabeth Kübler-Ross

Earthquake 1994

I HAD BEEN deep in sleep, dreaming that I was riding a train, racing through the night. My head hung out the window, enjoying the wind whipping against my face and the exhilaration surging through me. It was the kind of dream that made you feel alive. A voice, frantic and urgent, dragged me out of it.

"GET UP! IT'S AN EARTHQUAKE—A STRONG ONE," I heard Pete, my husband, yell, his words edged with panic.

I bolted upright, my heart hammering. My first instinct was to reach for my glasses—I'm blind without them—but my hand fumbled in the dark, grasping nothing. The earth convulsed beneath me. The bed rocked violently, skidding across the floor, blocking the doorway of our small room. My mind spun; my thoughts scattered. *My girls!* Where were they?

Just hours before, I had fallen asleep in the baby's room, curled around her as she drifted off. Now, in chaos, I frantically patted the bed until my hands found her. My gut clenched—her tiny body dangled precariously off the edge, her head hanging over the side. With shaking hands, I yanked her close, clutching her as if I could shield her from the rumbling tremors.

She stirred, opened her eyes, cupped my face in her chubby hands with tenderness, smiled sweetly, and said, "You silly Mommy, don't be afraid."

I really wanted to believe her.

Still barefoot, I reached for my slippers, but they were lost in the darkness. I grabbed a blanket instead, wrapping it around us as my husband reached for our older daughter. She was already awake and calmer than I could have imagined—much calmer than me. Clutching her doll and blanket, she stood in the doorway.

"Mom, come here! We need to stand under the doorway."

Little did she know that the frame above her door had fractured. The structure she trusted was moments away from collapsing onto us.

The shaking subsided long enough for a new fear to rise: the acrid scent of gas seeped into the room. Pete caught it too. In an instant, he was gone, running to shut off the main valve before it ignited.

"Get out of the house," he shouted. "I'll get the dog and the car."

We ran, the baby in my arms, my older daughter clinging to my side, our faces buried in blankets. My vision swam in the darkness—I still had no glasses. Then pain—sharp and searing—shot up from my foot. Glass. Blood. I gritted my teeth and pushed forward until we were outside.

Pete reappeared near the garage. "I can't find him!" he said, breathless.

He opened the garage door and stepped inside. Everything had collapsed onto the car. Our carefully arranged shelves had emptied themselves in the chaos, burying our car under our own belongings.

Outside, on the sidewalk, I tightened my hold on my girls, one in my arms, the other hugging my legs. The air hummed with the eerie stillness that follows a disaster. I tried to steady my voice—to reassure them. To reassure myself.

"It's okay. It'll stop soon."

But the earth wasn't finished.

Another tremor struck, shaking the ground beneath us. Then—like an act of mercy or a miracle—the quaking knocked away enough debris for Pete to squeeze into the car. He threw it in reverse, backing into the street just as the remaining boxes crashed down, spilling their contents across the driveway.

I turned, taking in the wreckage—our life in pieces.

"It doesn't matter," Pete said gently. "They're just things. We need to go. I'm not sure if the gas is fully shut off—I don't know what will happen. We can't stay here."

I scanned our surroundings, but everything blurred into indistinct shapes.

"What about the neighbors? Their houses?" I wanted to know.

Pete let out a dry chuckle. "They seem fine."

It wasn't until we drove away that I fully realized that while our house stood battered and broken, the homes on either side of our street were untouched. And no one else was outside in their pajamas except us. It was as if the quake had singled us out.

I fought the urge to scream. How was this possible? Was I trapped in a dream? Why only our house?

When we reached my mother's house five miles away, it was like stepping into another world. Everything was calm and quiet. Unable to see past the tip of my nose, my older daughter grabbed my hand and led me into the house.

My mother greeted us with a smile. "Did you feel the quake?" she asked, almost casually.

"Did I feel it?" My voice was uncertain, my mind struggling to reconcile the chaos we had fled with the serenity and stillness before me. "Were *you* scared?"

My mother shook her head. "God is protecting me. It wasn't bad at all. I stood under the doorway like they told us to, and it stopped."

It felt like a blessing that an elderly woman's house would remain untouched by the chaos. Her house was pristine. Nothing had moved, dropped, or broken.

I swallowed hard and finally let myself feel the pain in my foot. Blood had soaked through the blanket I had used to press against it. At least here, I could clean the wound— and find shoes. But my glasses were still missing. So, I borrowed my sister's contact lenses. They were too weak for my prescription, but I reminded myself that beggars can't be choosers.

Pete promised he would go back to our house when the tremors stopped for my glasses and to find our dog.

That night, as the shaking stopped, we left the girls with my mother and went back home.

Pete went in search of my glasses and found them in our bedroom—waiting, unbroken.

I headed to the backyard when I saw *him*.

Our dog lay motionless by the sliding glass door, his body unnervingly still. I called out his name. He didn't stir. A weight pressed against my chest.

I stepped closer, reached out, and touched fur that was far too cold.

He was gone.

I slid to the floor next to him. I wanted to wail, to curse, to rage against whatever force had spared the houses on either side of ours—but had taken my dog, my home, my children's sense of safety. But I could do nothing.

All I could do was stare at the little creature—who had brought so much joy to our family, especially to my girls— asleep forever.

Bubble. That was his name. We had found him in the first pet store that opened in the mall near us. Although we preferred to rescue and adopt animals, my older daughter had fallen in love with him at first sight. She even slept on the floor beside his bed the first night we brought him home. And Bubble loved her back with equal devotion—bounding toward her, leaping at her feet, making silly sounds only she could understand.

For eight years, he was her best friend. And now, I had to tell both my girls their sweet friend was gone.

Eventually, we rebuilt the house from the ground up, costing us more than we anticipated—but no amount of money could fix what had been broken inside us. The earthquake had reduced our home to rubble, but it had done twice as much damage to our mental well-being. It was the anguish and the intangible grief of losing our stability, our sense of self-preservation, and our security—the silent certainty that we were safe in the world—that lingered the most.

That, more than the house, took the longest to rebuild.

Renewed Beginnings

When you learn your lessons, the pain goes away.

—Dr. Elisabeth Kübler-Ross,
The Wheel of Life

On a Saturday morning, a beautiful, tall Black woman named Leetta walked into our clinic, clutching a cup of coffee. She asked to speak with a therapist about her work, and I was assigned to her. I was completing my doctorate at the time and rotating through a therapeutic clinic, where I treated patients under the supervision of experienced clinicians.

As part of my routine, I let new clients sit in the waiting room for a few minutes, observing their demeanor and assessing their anxiety. Leetta chose a chair, calmly sipping her coffee while gazing at the plain white wall. Despite her serene manner, there was a palpable sadness to her. I invited her into one of our counseling rooms to collect basic information before my supervisor joined us.

I gently asked, "What brings you here, Leetta?"

"I'm not sure if I'm burned out," she confessed, "but I no longer have the energy I once had to get up, get dressed, and go to work. I rely on stimulants," she gestured to her coffee, "to kickstart my day."

She explained that for the past two months, nothing had changed. For four years she had worked at a hospice near our clinic—a job she valued for its flexible hours and the close camaraderie with her colleagues. She mentioned that she rarely dated, saying men her age—mid-forties— preferred younger women who could party late into the night. Instead, she cherished her biweekly lunch outings with a couple of friends but avoided traveling with them, clinging to routine.

Over the next month, Leetta came to see me weekly, and I found her to be forthright, assertive, imaginative, and fiercely independent. She loved her work as a hospice nurse, though the constant loss of patients weighed heavily on her. She felt privileged to share in the final days of those she cared for, yet somehow the underlying source of her distress remained unspoken. When our conversations drifted to her future, she admitted she longed for a career that could provide financial security and a more stable life. She also revealed that her parents had died in a car accident when she was eight, leaving her to be raised by her grandmother.

In moments when words failed them, I often asked clients to share family photographs to help unlock their emotions.

"Do you have pictures of your family?" I asked one day.

Leetta hesitated at first, then retrieved four photographs from her purse.

"These are my parents," she said quietly. "I only recall a few Christmases together. Is it bad for me to say that?"

Still, there was one more photograph she kept hidden. With a mix of vulnerability and resolve, she finally showed me an image of a young girl with her grandmother. "This is my granny," she whispered. "I lost her five years ago. She was my favorite person—firm, determined, and wise. She taught me about life, integrity, and how to care for what I love."

Cradling the photograph, tears welled in her eyes. "I wasn't there when she died … She needed me, and I couldn't be there."

I offered gentle reassurance: "I'm sure she knew you would have been there if you could."

But in a sudden burst of anguish, Leetta shouted, "And I did the same thing to my patient recently!" and stormed out.

She missed our next session. When I called her later, she confided that work had completely overwhelmed her. A month passed before Leetta made an emergency call to me on a rainy weekend. I agreed to meet her in my office, but when she arrived, I hardly recognized the woman who had once carried herself like a model with proud vitality. The vibrant, poised Leetta had been transformed into someone broken—disheveled, depressed, exhausted, barely able to stand. Wearing a drab housedress, her hair unkempt and her face without makeup, she looked drained. She slumped onto the couch and bowed her head.

When I offered her a warm drink, she glanced up wearily and murmured, "Help … I need help."

That day she recounted the death of her patient a couple of weeks back, for whom she'd cared for nearly two years. Agatha—a woman with a heavy accent—was about the same age as Leetta's grandmother. In the early days, Agatha's family would visit frequently: first weekly, then biweekly, and eventually monthly. Her daughter and grandchildren would bring her food and gifts and have a small party in the backyard. Their visits had brought Agatha to life. But once the family left, she would slip back into silence.

One day, when Leetta had asked if there was anything she could do for Agatha, she had looked at Leetta and remarked, "Leetta? What kind of name is it?"

Laughing, Leetta had explained, "It's a made-up name. My granny Loretta combined her own name with my mother's, Darlene, to create Leetta."

Agatha had teased, "But there's no trace of Darlene—it seems like it's short for Loretta."

Leetta had admitted, "Yes, my granny never liked the name Darlene. At her mother-in-law's insistence, she named my mother Darlene, but when I was born, she took the two long e's from Darlene, inserted them into her own name, and transformed Loretta into Leetta. My granny thought it was very funny."

Agatha's laughter had softened the tension as she had added, "I would've liked your granny."

Prompted by a sudden hunch about Agatha's origins, Leetta had asked her what language she spoke with her children.

"Armenian," Agatha had replied. "Have you heard about Armenians?"

"Yes, of course—we even have three Armenian doctors here." Leetta had responded.

With a playful glint in her eye, Agatha had teased, "Are they married? My granddaughter is married to an *odar*."

When Leetta had questioned the term, Agatha had explained that *odar* meant "foreign" in Armenian, noting with a wink that her own grandson was unmarried.

In the weeks that followed, Leetta had many similar personal conversations with Agatha, who had gradually become more open about her life. Agatha had recounted the struggles of her family when they first moved to the United States—from the financial hardships of building a new home to confronting a society that viewed them as outsiders, all the while contending with the cultural pressures against mixed marriages.

On good days Agatha had been a delight, entertaining everyone in the lunchroom with anecdotes and singing soulful Armenian songs. The songs had touched Leetta, bringing tears to her eyes, even though she didn't understand the language. On bad days, however, Agatha was tormented by night terrors that left her breathless and screaming for God to take her away. Her medical team could only medicate her, leaving Leetta to watch helplessly.

Leetta had asked Agatha about those terrors, but she would either shut down or change the subject—until the night of April 24, 1996, when Agatha had finally broken her silence. She had described the horror of watching an Ottoman soldier torture and kill her grandmother. She had revealed to Leetta how the *Ganoderma*, meaning "a soldier" in Turkish, had dragged her mother away as she screamed for Agatha to run, to hide. At just seven years old, Agatha had fled blindly amidst the chaos she was witnessing: everyone was running, so she, too, had run and run. That night, Agatha had fallen asleep in Leetta's arms, sobbing—a sorrow no words Leetta could say that would ever console her.

Glancing around my office after relaying Agatha's story, Leetta took in my business card and certifications before asking, "You're Armenian?"

"Yes, I am," I confirmed.

"Are your grandparents alive?" she pressed.

"No, they're not. I know what you mean—like Agatha, I, too, carry the stories of the genocide. We cherish them so that our ancestors' sacrifices for our roots, language, religion, and culture will never be forgotten."

After our session ended and Leetta left, I reviewed my notes, trying to connect the dots between Leetta's depression, her anxiety, her work, and her unresolved grief over her grandmother. At our next meeting the following week, Leetta returned in the same somber mood as her first visit, sitting silently for several minutes. Being an unconventional therapist, I confronted her about her unwillingness to share more about her story.

In response, she began pacing, her voice rising as she confessed, "I feel guilty for having so many feelings for Agatha when my own grandmother isn't even here. I feel awful that I couldn't comfort my granny after all she endured with her own grandparents and the hardships of slavery. And most of all, I feel pathetic that one patient could affect me so deeply—I was trained as a nurse for being compassionate but not to become obsessed."

I smiled gently, and she noticed, asking, "What … What do you mean?"

I then inquired, "How did Agatha die?"

Leetta became subdued and sat down. Somberly, she lowered her head and cradled it in her hands.

"Her heart stopped …" she murmured. Leetta's emotions spilled over as she continued, "She told me to go and get some lunch. I had my lunch ready, but she insisted I step outside to feel the sun. It was a beautiful day, and she wanted me to let the warmth seep into my skin so she could feel it through me—through my hands … But by the time I returned … Agatha was gone. She had died … alone."

Her voice faltered, and she collapsed into the fetal position, crying silently as her body heaved unconsolably.

Overwhelmed by the weight of unexpressed grief—abandonment over her grandmother and sorrow for Agatha—Leetta confessed that she had never visited her grandmother's grave, even though she had ordered the tombstone.

Leetta gazed at me with pleading eyes, and without her having to ask, I offered, "I'll go with you."

We left the office and drove to the cemetery, a place that had always offered me a sense of peace and sanctuary. This one was no different. The grounds were beautifully maintained, with trees shading the graves and flowers scattered throughout.

I accompanied Leetta to a secluded corner where her grandmother's grave lay. There, she carefully set a small bouquet in the designated vase and gently touched the inscription:

Dearest Gran,
Loretta Mae Williams,
I will carry you with me
until I see you again.

In time, Leetta's overwhelming guilt gave way to healing. Through extensive work, she learned to embrace her grief— starting with the traditional practice of journaling, picking up hobbies, and joining a church choir. A year later, when she returned to my office, her demeanor was exactly the same as it was the day I met her: tall, confident, and happy. This time, she was accompanied by a four-year-old girl she had adopted.

The girl approached me, extended her little hand, and said brightly, "Hello, Doctor. My name is Loretta Mae Williams, and I was named after my great-grandmother. Nice to meet you!"

In that moment, I recognized the quiet transformation in Leetta—a testament to the enduring power of memory, healing, and new beginnings.

Embracing Loss

Dying is nothing to fear. It can be the most wonderful experience of your life. It all depends on how you have lived.

—Dr. Elisabeth Kübler-Ross

I HAVE THOUGHT about death since childhood. One moment we are conscious—alive, aware, breathing—the next, lifeless. It is a fact both mesmerizing and terrifying. My fascination with death began at the age of seven, sparked by my grandmother's tale about how I was named. Nene often told me the story of my birth and how a mere name altered my destiny. It was a name that rewrote my fate.

I was born the third female in my family, in a culture that revered male heirs—I was meant to be a boy, the third attempt at securing a son. My mother took good care of herself during her pregnancy with me—taking supplements, resting, and allowing herself to be pampered for the full nine months. But my birth brought unimaginable disappointment, especially for my father. Never loving toward my mother, he left home, vowing never to return. Feeling inadequate, my mother cried for days.

Amid family involvement steeped in tradition, my father returned and named me Esther. My Nene explained that before my father was born, my paternal grandmother had three daughters, each named Esther, who died in infancy—one at a year old, another at three months, and the last at birth. Longing for a son, my father believed that naming me Esther would doom me to the same fate.

But my Nene, with a spark of defiance, declared: "Don't worry, *aghchigs*—my daughter, I vow never to call you by that name. Everyone will call you Maral." In that simple name change lay the redirection of an ill fortune.

That moment also marked my first encounter with death. I began to imagine what being dead might involve. Would I feel anything? Would it hurt? Could I see my family again? What came after? My Sunday school teacher told us that if we were good, we would go to heaven and meet Jesus. I wondered what Jesus would be like, fretting over whether my own goodness was enough. How much "good" did it take? What if I wasn't good enough? The idea of eternal punishment—burning in hell without turning to ashes— haunted me. Thus began my lifelong obsession with being a good human—a desperate effort to outwit fate once sealed by a name.

My second encounter with death was a lesson etched into my soul. During the Armenian Genocide in 1915, the Ottoman soldiers butchered my Nene's mother. Every April 24, we heard about that gruesome story—a solemn ritual to keep alive the memory of the atrocities inflicted upon our ancestors, to carry the torch of remembrance with us. Even though it was a story fit for an entire book, at such a young age, it consumed my every thought.

I remember asking my Nene, "When I die, will your mom and dad recognize me? Will they be able to take care of me?"

With the characteristic firmness of a no-nonsense woman, she brushed aside my fears: "Those are useless thoughts. I need you to forget them."

Little did she know that those questions had first taken shape when she recounted the story of how I was named.

My third encounter with death came during a visit to my great aunt—affectionately called Tata—who lived in Der-Zor, a desert city in Syria near the Iraqi border. There, the Euphrates River flows silently through a landscape scarred by genocide. This very river holds an integral part of Armenian history: it witnessed the horrors of genocide—the countless deaths, where women, desperate to escape torture, plunged themselves and their children into the waters. Tata, with a steady gaze and an outstretched finger, pointed toward the river and warned, "*Never forget* many of your ancestors died here, including my precious mother and her unborn child."

Then came my fourth—and most poignant—encounter with death, through my friendship with Nadia, a girl around my age. Nadia's fragile health was evident during our last playdate. Pale, tired, and weak, she confided, "My head hurts a lot. Sometimes, I have to close my eyes because the light hurts." I tried to soothe her, but she withdrew into a quiet corner, seeking solace in sleep.

As I sat beside her, holding her hand, she opened her eyes briefly and said softly, "Can you give me the elephant?"

The small toy—crafted from a white jade-like material—was one I cherished from my visits to her house. Unlike most girls who played at being moms and keeping house, we imagined riding the elephant in faraway lands.

After I fetched it for her, she pressed the toy in my palm and whispered, "I want you to keep it safe. I don't want anyone else playing with it."

I protested lightly, "But what about you? You love it!"

Yet she fell silent, and I watched her, concerned, before calling out for her mother, who came and carried her to bed.

I left the elephant behind that day, hoping it would be there, waiting for our next playdate. But Nadia's health declined sharply. Tata later explained that Nadia had been hospitalized, though they expected her to recover and return home soon. When I saw her again, her beautiful, shiny brown hair had been shaved off—a necessary sacrifice to diagnose the cause of her persistent headaches.

Nadia lay on a makeshift bed on the floor, and when our eyes met, she murmured, "You didn't take the elephant."

"I want it to stay here," I told her. "So that we can both play with it when I come."

She gazed at me for a while, not replying. In that silent exchange, I sensed that Nadia would never be the same—and that soon, she would vanish from my life. I said nothing to her mother that evening, knowing with a heavy heart that I would never see Nadia again.

At the end of August, on a sunny day, Tata woke me with the somber news: Nadia had gone to heaven, and we were to visit her mother. I begged to stay home, unwilling to face a house empty without her, but Tata insisted. Reluctantly, I followed her to Nadia's second-floor home.

Peering inside, I saw women dressed entirely in black, wailing in despair, beating their breasts, and slapping their legs. I looked at Tata. She gave me a wordless signal urging me to remain quiet. I kissed Nadia's mom goodbye and stepped outside, sinking onto the stairs, overwhelmed with sadness.

I wondered why I wasn't crying. Though Nadia and I only saw each other during the summers, she was one of the few souls I trusted with my thoughts and feelings. I eventually dozed off until Tata's gentle touch on my shoulder reminded me it was time to go home. Then, unexpectedly, Nadia's mother emerged, took my hand, and placed the toy elephant into my palm before closing it. Kissing my forehead, she whispered, "Keep my baby alive with you."

I clung to that elephant until we moved to the United States. It shattered while we were packing, and my mother, unaware of its significance, discarded it. I was devastated and filled with lingering anger at my mother for a long time.

Nadia was my first profound personal loss—a goodbye I never got to say, and a gratitude I never expressed for the trust she had placed in me.

So, here it is, Nadia, wherever you may be: thank you for being a friend and a courageous young lady.

Serenity Steps

A f***ing new beginning.

We need to teach the next generation of children from day one that they are responsible for their lives. Mankind's greatest gift, also its greatest curse, is that we have free choice. We can make our choices built from love or from fear.

—Dr. Elisabeth Kübler-Ross

MY SISTER SONIA and I shared everything. Four years older than me, she was my idol, mentor, and true kindred spirit.

Sonia immigrated to the United States at nineteen, a year before we did, shouldering the burden of starting a new life for our family. She took this responsibility seriously—planning her education, working full-time, and preparing a home for us. Ambitious and driven, she had set her sights on accomplishing everything she wanted in life before turning thirty.

Her letters arrived every month, brimming with hope and determination. Initially expected to follow in my father's footsteps to study dentistry, Sonia changed her plans after settling in America. Weighing the time, effort, and expense of attending dental school, she switched her major to business and chose to pursue finance. This brave decision sent shockwaves through our family, causing upheavals.

My father saw it as a failure and a betrayal—after all, we came from a long lineage of dentists on both sides of the family. But Sonia was unbothered by his fury. She was eager to experience life on her own terms. She wanted to travel, see the world, learn a dozen languages, and embrace every adventure—both the highs and lows of life. Fearless, she spoke to everyone and befriended anyone—an embodiment of *joie de vivre*.

The Trip—One Year Later

OUR MOVE TO the United States brought unanticipated challenges. A year after Sonia left, my mother, my little sister Jules, and I packed our bags and set off to join her. My mother, then forty-three, was a beautiful woman with golden-brown hair, sparkling brown eyes, and a fair, translucent complexion. Though she was fluent in French, Armenian, Arabic, and Turkish, her English was limited. At fourteen, I could read English well but was too shy to speak it.

Before the trip, I was tasked with looking after Jules—a role I had assumed since her birth. We were apprehensive about the journey, burdened by its protocols and responsibilities, and quite literally weighed down by so much jewelry that we looked like Christmas trees. My mother had been advised not to pack our jewelry in the luggage, so we wore it instead. Jules and I had to wear long-sleeved shirts and turtlenecks in the dead heat of summer just to keep it hidden.

I was devastated to leave my hometown and my friends. I clung to the thought that I would never see them again, never forge such close relationships. Moving to a strange country with unfamiliar languages and customs was unbearable—I resented it. My only consolation was reuniting with my beloved sister. I was so consumed by my own sorrow that I neglected to ask Jules how she felt about the move. Years later, when I did, she barely remembered what had happened or how she had felt.

My mother knew. She kept looking at my tear-filled eyes and saying, "We will have a great life there, you will see." And if that didn't work, she would grow frustrated and say, "Stop it. Stop looking back. This is happening—it's happening now."

Our first immigration stop was Frankfurt, Germany. A tall, stern-faced officer scrutinized our Syrian passports, then began questioning my mother. Why was she traveling alone? Where was her husband? What was her destination, and why? Initially, my mother responded calmly, explaining that we were Armenians, not Arabs, and that traveling without a husband was customary. But as the interrogation dragged on, her composure faltered.

My mother informed them she didn't know German or English and asked for a translator in one of the four languages she spoke. None were available. The officers led her away to a windowless room. When my sister and I tried to follow, they stopped us, refusing to let us go with her.

My mother protested, insisting she couldn't leave her two underage daughters alone, and demanded she be permitted to call her brother, who was waiting for us in Denmark. But they ignored her pleas and ushered us into another room, leaving her in tears.

I gathered the courage to ask in English, "What's going on?"

"Do you know English? You must translate," one officer said—only for another to immediately object. He waved his arms dismissively and ordered us to be taken away.

My sister and I were locked in a cold, barren room with gray walls and two chairs. Jules whimpered, her voice breaking. "Where is Mom? I want to be with her. Why did they take Mom to jail? Are we going to jail too?" She sobbed again and again. "I want Mom."

I tried to stay calm, but my heart raced with fear. "Mom is not in jail," I tried to reassure my little sister—though I wasn't sure I believed it myself. "We haven't done anything wrong. They just need to ask her some questions."

An hour later, Jules got fidgety again. "I need to pee," she said.

I tried opening the door, but it was locked. I knocked, but no one answered. I searched the room for a phone or a call button to alert the officers that we needed help but found neither. Desperate, I banged on the door and shouted until, at last, an officer opened it, barking what sounded like obscenities in German.

"My sister needs to pee," I said firmly in English.

They motioned her to come alone, but I refused to let her go without me. My insistence irritated them. One officer muttered angrily, gesturing for both of us to follow.

I was surprised to find someone else waiting for us when Jules was done. A kind female officer—her demeanor gentler than the others—met us outside and escorted us back to the windowless room.

"Do you need anything?" she asked in English.

"Yes, please. My sister is hungry, and I need water," I answered.

After what felt like an hour since she left and locked the door, it finally opened. Suddenly, a familiar face appeared. My uncle, his expression a mixture of relief and concern, pulled us into a tight hug, making Jules cry again.

"Are you okay?" he asked.

"Where is Mom?" I demanded.

"She's still in the other room, but she'll be done soon."

"Why are they holding her?"

"I'll explain later."

Within minutes, the kind officer returned, handing Jules a sandwich and me a small bottle of water. My uncle reassured us again that everything would be fine. I turned away as Jules ate, not wanting her to see the tears rolling down my face.

Another hour crawled by before the door opened again. The kind officer took us by the hand and led us to our mother, who sat in a chair, her flushed face, a storm of emotions. She was waving her hands angrily, furiously, at my uncle, her voice filled with frustration. The moment Jules saw her she ran forward, clutching her tightly, sobbing.

"Don't leave us alone again," she begged.

My mother wrapped her arms around her and whispered soothing words. "Everything is fine. We're leaving soon."

By then, we had missed our connecting flight, our plan delayed by the ordeal. My uncle secured another one to Denmark, where we stayed for a month before finally making our way to the United States.

Made in the USA

OUR JOURNEY WAS long but filled with anticipation. I remember thinking: *I will see my soulmate Sonia again—my sister, whom I adore. I can't wait to hear about her adventures and stories. Life will be good!*

"Welcome to Los Angeles, California—the Golden State," announced the captain.

We took a taxi from the airport to the San Fernando Valley. Looking around, I felt like I'd stepped into an old cowboy movie: rows of small cottage-like houses, trees everywhere, and stores with unfamiliar names like Ralphs and Vons, scattered at random. The streets were impeccably clean, filled with cars, yet eerily empty of pedestrians.

We were used to curfews—what was called *mamnough tajaol* in Arabic—where being out at certain times was forbidden, a common practice back home especially during the war. I turned to my uncle and asked if there was such a curfew. He chuckled and said, "No, we are not in a war zone, but no one walks here. We drive."

Back in Damascus, amid the conflict, the city pulsed with energy. The streets buzzed with lively conversations and laughter. You could stroll down the streets, past beautiful condominiums with penthouses—similar to the one we used to live in—and wander directly into vast parks where everyone gathered. Ice cream was bought at one stand, flowers at another. Life was vibrant there.

The emptiness of the deserted streets unsettled me, crushing the image I had of America. I looked over at Sonia, and she knew exactly what I was thinking. She smiled and said, "We're in the suburbs. All the homes are tiny one-story houses. People don't walk. They drive everywhere."

Over the next eleven months, Sonia became my guide to this strange new world, teaching me cultural norms and showing me around. She even taught me how to drive her little red VW Bug—a stick shift that I never quite mastered.

I also struggled with the culture of the private school my mother had enrolled us in. So, I decided to take the GED exam instead and planned to start at Valley College in the fall. Sonia, who worked there as a student assistant while taking morning classes, let me shadow her three days a week. The rest of the time, I helped my mother at home.

I cherished every moment with Sonia, journaling everything I saw and heard. My English improved as she patiently corrected my pronunciation. Every morning on our way to college, she would crack jokes, making me laugh until I cried. Life was beginning to feel beautiful again.

Then, on Wednesday, June 23, 1976, everything changed.

Sonia came home for lunch and casually mentioned that she was going sailing with her instructors—but she wasn't planning to tell Mom. I objected immediately. It seemed dangerous, especially since she had never sailed before and barely knew her instructors. My concern irritated her.

"You're too young," she snapped, annoyed at my meddling. "You have no right to tell me what to do with my life."

Her words stung and infuriated me. Furious, she grabbed her purse and left.

I tried to distract myself by watching TV. *Gone with the Wind* was airing at 7:00 p.m.—a movie Sonia had recommended because it was easier to follow than reading the book. Just as I settled in, the phone rang, and I picked it up. A voice on the other end introduced himself as a police officer.

"How old are you?" he asked.

A ridiculous question, I thought, but answered, "Fifteen."

"Do you know Sonia?"

"She is my sister."

There was a pause. Then, he asked, "Is there an adult I can speak to?

I handed the phone to Uncle Albert, the only adult at home, and went back to my movie, annoyed by the interruption. A few minutes later, he walked in, turned off the TV, and told me to get ready. We were leaving.

How rude—I was watching my movie! my mind shouted. But I didn't argue. I got ready, then went out to the car. I sat there, waiting for him to explain. As he started the engine, he finally spoke, not looking at me.

"Sonia had a car accident. We're going to the hospital."

"Wait … she wears contacts!" I cried out. "I need to bring her glasses so she can see. And extra clothes. Did they know to take out the contacts?"

He nodded.

My mind raced, *She's alive. She must be. It must have been a small accident. She'll be home soon. She'll be fine, right?*

My uncle said nothing. His silence offered no reassurance, leaving my unspoken question hanging between us.

Encino Hospital was a small, specialized facility. As we arrived, I noticed the absence of the usual hospital smells—a mixture of Lysol, alcohol, and medication. Uncle Albert led me to the ICU, which I later learned stood for Intensive Care Unit.

In the waiting room, my mother sat in a chair, wailing, demanding to see Sonia. My uncles, Albert and Berj, paced in and out, while Sarkis sat beside her. Overwhelmed, I struggled to make sense of their hushed, urgent conversations. Uncle Albert nudged me toward my mother, urging me to comfort her, but I didn't know how. More than anything, I needed to know when Sonia would be well enough to go home.

She had to be okay—right?

I heard Uncle Sarkis murmur to my mother, "I had a dream last night. The house you just bought collapsed, but a hand lifted it up again. Everything will be fine—don't worry."

Uncle Berj, still pacing, finally turned to me. "Come," he said. "I'll take you to see Sonia."

He warned me that she was unconscious, hooked up to machines, and covered in tubes. His words didn't fully register—my mind was spinning. "Now listen," he repeated, "she's not conscious. So, don't be alarmed by all the tubes."

The room was narrow, filled with beeping machines and a tangle of wires. Sonia's small body was barely visible among them. My uncle held my shoulders, stopping me from rushing to her side. I just wanted to talk to her.

"They removed all her clothes," I whispered, noticing part of her body exposed. "She'll catch a cold. I need to cover her."

A nurse overheard and gently adjusted the blanket.

"She is in a coma," Uncle Berj said. "She can't hear you."

I fought back tears as he pulled me away.

"But I hardly saw her," I protested. "I need more time."

"Not now," he said. "They need to take care of her."

And just like that, I was driven home, reassured by my uncles that it was for the best, that Sonia was in good hands.

That night, I lay in Sonia's bed, unable to sleep. The hospital scene replayed in my mind like an endless loop. Around

1:00 a.m., exhaustion finally overtook me—until I jolted awake.

I felt Sonia standing at the end of the bed, smiling at me.

I rubbed my eyes. She was gone.

Panic surged through me. I opened a window to catch my breath. Then, it dawned on me—I had to know she was alive! I grabbed the phone and asked the operator to connect me to the ICU at Encino Hospital.

A soft, feminine voice answered, "Can I help you?"

"Yes, I need to know if my sister, Sonia, is alive."

Silence.

"Hello," I pleaded. "She was in an accident yesterday. I need to know if she's alive."

"I'm sorry, ma'am, but we cannot give that information over the phone."

I swallowed hard. "Are you telling me she's … not?"

"How old are you, ma'am?"

Not my age again! my mind screamed.

"I'm old enough," I replied, demanding with a shaky voice, "just tell me if she's alive."

A pause. "Please hold."

Minutes later, the voice returned. "Yes, she is."

"Thank God," I whispered.

Thursday, June 24, 1976

I WOKE UP early, preparing to head to the hospital, when I noticed my mother, my uncles, and other relatives gathered in our home. My mother, supported by my uncles, sat on the couch near the door, her expression distant, her body heavy with medication. My grandparents and several family members moved about the house with quiet purpose— making coffee, preparing food, and serving water.

My grandmother caught my Uncle John's eye. He gestured for me to follow him. "Come with me to the backyard," he said. "I have something important to tell you."

I followed him to the far end of the yard, my heart pounding. He took my hands, his grip firm yet gentle.

"I need you to be strong," he said. "You have your mother and little sister to care for. Sonia has passed away."

"No," I whispered. "I know she didn't. I called the hospital—they told me she was alive."

"Listen to me," he insisted. "She is gone."

"NO!" I screamed, my voice raw, my hands shaking as I struggled against his hold. "I NEED TO GO TO HER."

A sudden, sharp slap stung my cheek, jolting me into silence. My vision blurred, my legs buckled, and I sank to the ground despite my uncle's grip on me.

"I will leave you here for a little while," he mumbled. "I'll come back for you."

I lay there on the concrete floor of the patio, the heat pressing into my skin. My body shook uncontrollably as I sobbed in silence, without tears.

The next three months passed in a thick haze. I moved through each day mechanically, doing only what was necessary. Every night, the scene at the hospital replayed in my mind like a horror movie I couldn't erase.

One of the hardest things I had to do was go through Sonia's belongings, deciding whether to keep her clothes or read her papers. Among them, I found a journal entry detailing her greatest fear: being buried alive. She wrote of the panic, the claustrophobia, the desperate screams for help—unheard, unanswered. Reading her words, I was horrified. The thought consumed me.

Shaking, I asked my uncles if she had been aware, trapped in her wounded body as she lay in that hospital bed. They dismissed my fears, assuring me that Sonia had been brain-dead upon arrival at the hospital and that her heart had stopped later. Perhaps to an adult, their explanation would have been logical. But to a teenager, already drowning in fear and helplessness, it became an unbearable weight. Anxiety morphed into full-blown panic attacks that haunted me for years.

I took care of my mother, managed the house, and fulfilled my responsibilities to survive, but I never truly mourned my precious sister. Over time, memories blurred, and one day, her voice faded away. What remained vivid, however, was the image of her lifeless face, her fragile body in the ICU, and the bitter sting of our final argument just hours before her accident. Those memories never faded.

I've been through therapy twice in my life, once during my school days and again, when I lost most of my memory after an unexplained seizure. Through memory therapy, I regained fragments of the past—more than I had anticipated or desired. But among the resurfaced memories was the sound of Sonia's voice. I could hear my sister again.

I knew I should have gone to grief therapy, but life's obligations always took precedence. In its place, I honored Sonia in my own way. I named my firstborn after her, though I couldn't bring myself to say her name for years. Instead, I called my little girl *Joudig*—"tiny chick" or "little bird" in Armenian. Joudig doesn't look like Sonia, but certain gestures—the way she speaks quickly, her sarcasm, and most of all, her ability to find goodness in everything—are pure Sonia.

Then, as luck would have it, my second daughter, Niki, came along. She, too, doesn't resemble Sonia physically, but she carries her intelligence and wisdom. And when Niki laughs from the heart—when her nose wrinkles, her big eyes squint, and her entire face radiates joy—I hear Sonia. The same sound. The same voltage. The same energy.

Nearly fifty years ago, I left my comfortable life, seeking adventure and opportunity in a new country. I never imagined that I would befriend my sorrows and that they would become a part of who I am. I never sought recovery from my grief—I feared that moving on and letting go would mean losing my sister all over again. So, I cradled my grief like a baby, carried it with me, and took consolation in it—so I would never forget my sister in my bliss.

Forty-eight years later, I still grieve her. Every single day.

Hopeful Hearts

—⁂—

The most beautiful people we have known are those who have known defeat, known suffering, known struggle, known loss, and have found their way out of the depths. These persons have an appreciation, a sensitivity, and an understanding of life that fills them with compassion, gentleness, and a deep loving concern. Beautiful people do not just happen.

—Dr. Elisabeth Kübler-Ross,
Death: The Final Stage of Growth

The Story of Sam

I CARRY A lot of emotional baggage about raising Sam. Growing up, having children was never on my agenda. In my chaotic world, juggling marriage and motherhood was never part of the dream. Witnessing my parents' disastrous marriage, I doubted my ability to marry or parent. Even when I married, I didn't expect it to last—or for children to follow.

To my delight, I relished my nine-month pregnancy with Sam, experiencing many firsts—but none more surprising than the two that stood out. First, I suddenly became the center of attention. As the third child, I had always lived in the shadows, so being in the spotlight was confusing but delightful. The second "first" was the pregnancy "glow." For the first time, I was called beautiful—an adjective I had never associated with myself. I had always been seen as intelligent, level-headed, and poised—but never beautiful.

For eight and a half months, the little embryo Sam was silent as a mouse. At times, I wondered if she was even alive. I lost a lot of weight but felt great. Sam was born two weeks early, weighing six pounds, four ounces, and measuring nineteen inches. When they brought her to me, panic overwhelmed me as I realized I held her future in my hands—without knowing what to do or how to do it right. An experienced nurse saw my frightened face and said, "It will come to you, just love her."

The following twelve months were among the most challenging of my life. I formed an intense bond with my baby—powerful, as any attachment between two human beings—but I also battled the worst case of postpartum depression. At that point in my life, I hadn't finished my schooling, earned my degree, or found work that would allow me to provide the best for this little creature I'd brought into an unpleasant world. My many unfinished plans only intensified my anxiety.

When Sam turned one, I had to start working because we were struggling financially. I left her with my mother, who was also working from home while caring for her own parents and my demanding father. Every morning, I rose early, bundled Sam up with her favorite doll, and drove to my mother's house. Little Sam gazed at me, her eyes filled with understanding that I was about to drop her off and leave her behind. She'd cry the moment I parked in front of my mother's house.

No matter how many promises I made, kisses I gave, or bribes I offered, she cried when I left. I would glance in the rearview mirror and see her tiny hands outstretched, as if calling my name. And so, my hour-and-a-half drive to work was filled with tears and self-loathing.

When Sam was two, a friend suggested that I enroll her in a nursery. She loved it so much that, for the first time, she woke up excited to be dropped off. Unfortunately, that happiness was short-lived. The nursery closed before the year was out, and subsequent placements were disastrous. Eventually, we returned to the familiar routine at my mother's house.

Sam hated change. She was always afraid I might abandon her, growing wary and cautious around every new person—a reaction I felt responsible for. Her Pre-K years were generally happy; she enjoyed school, and the teachers adored her. Yet, no one ever praised her intelligence. I was constantly told that she was shy and not yet ready for schoolwork. Determined to help, I made a concerted effort to teach her at night—reading to her and asking her questions. But it soon became clear that my little girl didn't appreciate the inquiries. She would withdraw when I asked about school, happiest when left alone at home, surrounded by her Barbies and toys.

As Sam grew older, she struggled academically. Her performance faltered, and her teachers seemed to have given up on her. Having just finished my master's program in psychology, I recognized her withdrawal as a sign of distress and decided to take her to work with me. At my desk, she behaved like a little lady—poised, proper, and pleasant—and quickly became a hit with my colleagues and patients. I soon noticed she had difficulty with coloring and counting, and it became clear that Sam was dyslexic.

I presented my diagnosis to her teachers, explaining, "I evaluated her at work, and she appears to be dyslexic with a mild attention disorder." Her homeroom teacher replied, "I don't see it. She doesn't like to do the work. She's quiet in class and a bit lazy. I know you're her mother, but let's not make excuses for her. All she needs is a little discipline and tutoring."

My frustration grew, and I tried to change her school several times. But Sam was deeply attached to her friends and begged me not to move her. I yielded to appease her. Tutoring soon became a regular part of our routine. In addition to my sister and me, I enlisted paid tutors and teachers. Over time, Sam overcame her difficulties and blossomed into a generous, sociable young lady during her teenage years. She volunteered for numerous nonprofits and eagerly seized every opportunity to make a positive impact on her community.

At the school's final parent-teacher conference before graduation, the Chair of the History Department, shamelessly remarked: "You know, she will never go to college. She will be a good wife."

I will forever remember that backhanded compliment as one of the worst moments of my life. I made it my mission to instill in Sam that marriage should not define her, that her career and safety must take priority, and—most importantly—that she was an intelligent woman capable of achieving anything she set her mind to.

Despite all my many failings, Sam turned out to be balanced, beautiful, and benevolent. She excelled during her college years, earning a degree in Interior Architecture and securing a job with the company where she interned—steadily climbing the corporate ladder ever since.

Sam dedicated herself to working hard to achieve her goals and meet everyone's expectations. She studied diligently and worked even harder. As the youngest—and a woman in a business dominated by men—she earned everyone's respect. Whenever she was promoted or recognized for her work, my heart filled with pride, joy, and tender admiration. The biblical phrase "my cup runneth over" hardly captured my emotions.

I always believed that if we wanted something badly enough, we could achieve it. Yet, I never considered the cost. Hard-won success often comes at the expense of life's simple joys. I eventually realized that relentless effort has its own price. While Sam's friends sought romance, adventure, and fun, she devoted herself entirely to succeeding in the corporate world.

Sam Moves Out

I HAD ALWAYS expected Sam to move out when she got married, following the tradition in Armenian society. So, when she relocated to be closer to her work, I marked it as another first. I anticipated her leaving for school, yet I knew she would eventually return. But when she moved out with all her belongings—her bed, books, and albums—my heart sank into a void of hopelessness. I had to accept that she had established her own home—and that I was no longer part of it.

Years passed quickly, and our family situation changed several times—up and down. We changed houses, switched jobs, but always stayed close. Sam moved back a few times to help the family financially and emotionally, then moved out again. She seemed to move yearly—I wasn't sure if it was her restlessness or the family's circumstances.

Before I knew it, we were celebrating Sam's thirtieth birthday. Our family crisis had eased into a calmer phase, though we were still emotionally drained. It was then that I realized how well my husband, Zed, and I had raised our daughters. Nita, my second born and ten years younger than Sam, had just finished college and was already thriving as a Physician Associate. Life seemed to have settled, but fate had more in store for us.

"I need to freeze my eggs," Sam announced casually one day, walking through the living room. "My gyno told me I should freeze my eggs."

I frowned, quickly brushing aside the idea. "Many people have children after thirty."

"My tests showed very low levels of the hormone responsible for fertility," she said, frustration edging her voice.

I hesitated. "It might be a good idea to get a second opinion."

"For the love of God, Mom, why don't you accept that this could be a problem for me in the future? I might not be able to have kids!" Sam cried, her voice trembling as her eyes filled with tears.

That moment did it for me: in an instant, she was my five-year-old little girl again—straight, shiny black hair, thick bangs, rosy cheeks, and golden flecks shining brightly in her big brown, anime-like eyes. It was especially poignant when those eyes filled with tears, and my heart melted all over again. I rushed to her and hugged her tightly. She gently pulled away, but I longed to rewind time—to when she was more open to my wisdom and affection, when she believed I could fix anything with just a phone call.

"I hope you meet someone special, someone who sweeps you off your feet," I said, my voice thick with emotion. "I hope you marry him and have lots of kids. But until then, I will support whatever you decide to do and stand by you through it all." My words came out in a lump, as I fought back my own tears.

At the dinner table, Zed and Nita, potential grandpa and aunt, joked about naming the babies *Khosrof* and *Khosrofouhi*. Sam laughed, joining in on their playful stories, her face lighting up. I smiled at her, but then caught her wistful, melancholic gaze. My chest tightened, and I rushed to the bathroom before she could see *my* tears—I couldn't hold them back any longer.

Soon after, we had an appointment with Dr. Benjamin, the specialist recommended by her gynecologist. The receptionist informed us that the consultation would cost $300 and emphasized that payment was made up front before filling out any paperwork. Dr. Benjamin escorted us to his imposing office, briefly reviewed the lab report, and then turned to Sam.

"What are you hoping to achieve?" he asked.

Sam explained that her gynecologist had advised her to freeze her eggs since she wasn't in a relationship yet, adding that I didn't agree with the decision.

He turned to me, his tone derisive. "And why do you object?"

"If she put as much effort into finding someone as she's putting into freezing her eggs, then having babies would be easier," I said. "Besides—"

He cut me off, turning back to Sam. "You're thirty-three years old," he said. "This is your decision to make. Here's what we'll do: I'll perform an ultrasound to check how many follicles we can extract. If we have three or four, we'll start injections next week and extract the eggs the following week. I'll also send you for more lab work."

He led us into the exam room, boasting about his clinic's top-tier storage facilities for frozen eggs—the best, he emphasized, in the San Fernando Valley. The room was equipped with an ultrasound machine, a gynecological chair, and a pull-out drape. He motioned for me to sit on the opposite side of the room, away from Sam, who positioned herself awkwardly in the chair, tucking her feet in the stirrups.

Every woman knows the vulnerability—and the humiliation—of being in that chair. Legs apart, exposed, prodded by cold, unfamiliar instruments—gadgets and widgets intimidating enough to look at, let alone have inserted into your vagina. We endure it because we are women of the twenty-first century, we understand that prevention is the key to our health. Although I had taken my daughters to their first gynecological exams when they were young, seeing my grown daughter exposed to something far from preventive made me uneasy.

Dr. Benjamin, it seemed, didn't appreciate my presence. He didn't involve me in anything from that point onward. A long rod attached to the ultrasound machine was inserted into Sam, and she lay with her legs spread. I sat behind her, unable to see what was happening, hoping that Dr. Benjamin would at least explain what he was doing—walking her through the steps—so I could be part of the experience.

But to my disappointment, Dr. Benjamin remained silent until after he'd twisted the rod a few times, finally announcing, "We have two follicles on this side, and three on the other. It would be best, if you're willing to try again, as we need more follicles to get more eggs."

He left the room immediately after, instructing Sam to follow him. I stepped out to find her lost in thought. After a long silence, she spoke, "I don't have much chance with what I have. They need at least ten follicles to proceed.

Then, they'll choose the viable ones—probably half of that number. From that, we might get a few good eggs to freeze."

"So, what happens in your case?" I asked.

"Well, I don't know," Sam said, her voice faltering, her beautiful eyes welling up again.

"We need a second opinion!" I said, taking her hand and leading her out the door.

My sister and her husband recommended Dr. Ozerk. Over twenty years ago, they had struggled to conceive, and Dr. Ozerk had played a key role in their pregnancy, ultimately helping them have a beautiful daughter, Alexandra. Dr. Ozerk's office was warm and inviting, adorned with baby pictures and heartfelt notes from grateful parents. The room was filled with orchids, and I wondered if it was her birthday.

Dr. Ozerk was a young, soft-spoken woman with a calming presence. She listened intently as Sam explained that I wasn't comfortable with the procedure. Dr. Ozerk turned to me and said, "I understand that this feels unconventional for you, and it would have been ideal if everything had gone according to plan. But this is the reality we're facing, and we need to work with it. And who knows? Maybe by doing this, we'll send some positive energy into the universe for Sam to find someone, and then she will have it all."

I smiled, wondering if she was trying to charm me into supporting the decision.

The multiple IVF procedures to extract Sam's eggs were not only exceedingly expensive but also painful, complicated to witness, and physically demanding on her body. Yet she endured it all, triumphantly, and managed to freeze two eggs.

Time to Unfreeze

ONE OF THE hardest things that I had to witness was seeing my child suffer. This wasn't just about feeling bad or shedding tears because things weren't going as expected. Imagine the scenes from barbaric movies where the victim is tortured with various methods—physical and psychological—and you're standing there witnessing it, helpless, shackled, unable to move or speak. Every time Sam endured the physical demands of the procedures, the pain inflicted on her, the psychological toll she suffered afterward, and the endless stream of tears that followed, I felt bound by invisible shackles. Helpless and unable to offer a single word of reassurance, I couldn't reach out to soothe my child's pain.

A few years later, Sam decided it was time to try for a baby. She sought a new doctor after Dr. Ozerk unexpectedly sold her practice without informing Sam. A distant relative who was a fertility expert, Dr. Mathew, was recommended, so Sam drove thirty miles to see him. However, he wasn't optimistic about working with the frozen eggs and offered little hope. Still, Sam decided to proceed, since she'd been holding onto them for this very reason.

The first few days of fertilization in a petri dish went perfectly. On day one, both eggs grew, and we celebrated, laughing, convincing ourselves that good things were on the horizon. By day two, both eggs were fertilized and stable. We rejoiced again. By day three, the eggs were still growing, and the doctor was surprised at their progress, calling it a miracle when he shared the good news. It was then—only then—that we allowed ourselves to believe that a miracle was truly unfolding. The weekend arrived, and we were still celebrating the growth of those tiny nuggets of living cells.

Then Monday came, and Dr. Mathew delivered the dreaded news: the eggs had stopped growing. They were no longer viable and would need to be discarded.

For Sam, the world seemed to stop. It took time for joy, hope, and excitement to drain away, making room for overwhelming disappointment, desolation, and despair. She looked around but everything felt hollow. She listened to the doctor explaining the next steps, but it was as though she couldn't hear him.

In the past, she had always clung to a glimmer of hope, even when things seemed uncertain. That hope had grown stronger as the eggs were fertilized and began to develop, and for three days, Sam had been on cloud nine. Even as she slowly recovered from COVID, nothing mattered except those tiny nuggets growing. But now, everything had vanished. There were no eggs left, no partner to try again naturally, and no future in which she could carry a child.

Life Goes On

RECOVERING FROM COVID might give you a sense of triumph, but your body doesn't always feel the same. Sam's emotions were in turmoil after the disappointment of her eggs. I stayed with her, watching as she cycled through moments of crying, followed by attempts at normalcy— moving around silently, checking work messages, keeping busy with mundane tasks. When it was time for me to leave and return to my own reality, I held her tightly in my arms.

Without saying much, she looked at me with mournful, inconsolable eyes and told me, "I'll be okay, Mom. Don't worry."

I clung to her hand, unwilling to let go, remembering when she was young, and I comforted her in the same way.

I rushed out of her house, hiding my tears. But as I drove down the dreaded, traffic-congested 101 Freeway, I let out a sound I didn't recognize. I wanted to scream at God, to make my voice loud enough to be heard, but all that escaped was a soft grunt. My tears had dried up, my spirit drenched in sorrow, and my soul felt lost. I couldn't even fathom the depths of Sam's pain.

I encouraged Sam to seek therapy, which she eventually did. After a year, I could see that she was doing much better than I was. Her grief had become a part of her, and she had embraced it like a champion. It was as though she had wrapped those tiny nuggets tightly in a warm blanket inside her soul, holding them close as part of her forever.

Sadly, my younger daughter went through the same heart-wrenching experience a few years later. Watching my two daughters endure such devastating pain was incredibly difficult. These remarkable young women, who had done everything right, were suffering in a way that felt unjust—especially when conceiving a child came so easily for others. Once again, I found myself shackled by helplessness, unable to ease their pain. The grief of losing their dreams of becoming biological mothers will stay with them for years.

Every time they honor their friends' pregnancies and births, I watch them. They smile, seeming happy for their friends' blessings, but their smiles are always tinged with a melancholic yearning for what could have been.

PART TWO

Death and Grief

About Grief, Bereavement, and Mourning

WE ALL KNOW grief. We've all faced it in one form or other. Some have dealt with it quickly, some are still dealing with it, and some carry it like a badge of honor.

What is grief? The Merriam-Webster online dictionary broadly defines it as "deep and poignant distress caused by or as if by bereavement," typically involving the loss of a loved one through death. In psychological terms, the American Psychological Association's dictionary describes grief as "the anguish experienced after significant loss, usually the death of a beloved person," and distinguishes it from bereavement and mourning as follows:

> Not all bereavements result in a strong grief response, and not all grief is given public expression ... Grief often includes physiological distress, separation anxiety, confusion, yearning, obsessive dwelling on the past, and apprehension about the future. Intense grief can become life-threatening through disruption of the immune system, self-neglect, and suicidal thoughts. Grief may also take the form of regret for something lost, remorse for something done, or sorrow for a mishap to oneself.

In practical terms, grief is the experience of coping with loss—anything that disrupts our routine, our relationships, or our sense of self. It is an organic, natural response to loss, especially that of a loved one. Grief is a sophisticated, complex set of emotions influenced by cultural and religious beliefs, encompassing a range of experiences and behaviors.

We grieve with our five senses—sight, touch, hearing, smell, and taste. Whether joyful or traumatic, sensory experiences evoke powerful memories. The suffocating confinement of an abusive past, the cozy warmth of a blanket your mother tucked around you each night, the rich aroma and taste of your grandmother's cooking, or the lingering voice of a loved one in an old voice message—each can serve as a poignant trigger, bringing grief to the surface every time.

What Do We Grieve?

ANSWERING THIS QUESTION is both simple and profoundly complicated. We grieve the loss of anything or anyone meaningful to us. Yet, how we grieve is deeply personal. Despite being taught critical thinking from an early age, forming relationships in kindergarten, and learning ethics and integrity through work, no one ever prepares us for grief.

Most people are creatures of habit. From childhood, we follow routines that bring comfort and a sense of control over our emotions. We also learn early that death is inevitable—some more acutely than others, having faced loss at a young age. The death of someone close to us is one of the most profound experiences we will endure, yet we receive no guidance on how to navigate it.

Beyond the obvious losses—death from old age, accident, or illness—grief manifests in different forms. We mourn a colleague of fifteen years who is suddenly let go. A nurse who has cared for a patient daily—laughing and sharing stories—must say an abrupt goodbye one morning, like Leetta in "Renewed Beginnings." A beloved pet, a loyal companion, declines, and we must make the painful choice to end its suffering, as the mother describes in "Comforting Souls." Immigrants and refugees leave behind homes, friends, and everything familiar, grieving not only people but places and identities lost.

While writing this book, I discovered resources beyond the usual. One of the most impactful was Anderson Cooper's podcasts. I had never been drawn to podcasts or radio programs—I'm a visual person, and listening often sends my mind to places I'd rather not go. Yet, hearing Cooper's struggle with grief gave me relief. It reminded me that I am not alone in mourning my sister for so long and embracing grief as a companion, rather than something to "get over."

His conversations were educational, emotionally affirming, and fulfilling, revealing how others relate to this unique emotion of embracing grief—just as I do, by holding onto my sister's memory. I encourage anyone grieving to listen to them—you may find a friend and a kindred spirit. I rarely cry, but Andrew Garfield's words in his *Cooper* interview moved me to tears: "I hope the grief stays with me," he said, "because it's all the unexpressed love." His words resonated deeply. There was so much I still wanted to tell my sister, especially after our final conversation. Somehow, his sentiment validated my need to hold onto her memory.

For those who believe in God, suffering often raises the question: Why, God? In his conversation with Cooper, Stephen Colbert offered this answer: "If you are grateful for your life, you have to be grateful for all of it." Perhaps, like a marriage vow—for better or worse—we must learn to accept everything life brings.

My greatest fear after my sister's death was that she would be forgotten. And in many ways, she was. No one recalled memories or mentioned her name. The silence suffocated me. I wanted to scream that she mattered. However brief her time here, she left her mark. But with her absence, she could no longer assert herself, and I felt compelled to do it for her.

Unresolved grief silenced my family. We avoided speaking of her, afraid that doing so would bring sadness and tears. We needed to move on, we told ourselves. We needed to live.

On Death and Dying

The Stages of Dying

GRIEF AND MOURNING demand that we address death and dying. For those who have never experienced the death of a loved one, the end of life is often a morbid and uncomfortable topic. It is the unspoken certainty that many try to ignore.

Others—like me, who have witnessed it too often—tend to talk about it constantly. My daughters roll their eyes whenever I mention my own mortality. I ensured my daughters attended their grandparents' funerals—willingly, of course—because I wanted them to understand the process. Perhaps I overdid it. Though this exposure may have heightened their awareness, it can't shield them from grief, because they have also learned to love. And love is eternal.

Renowned psychiatrist Dr. Elisabeth Kübler-Ross, one of the foremost thinkers on death and dying, stressed in her work that humans are inherently designed to live—and to die. She believed that much of the grief and trauma associated with death stems from a lack of understanding about the process.

She also argued: "We need to teach the next generation of children from day one that they are responsible for their lives. Humanity's greatest gift, also its greatest curse, is that we have free choice. We can make our choices built from love or fear."

Her most significant contribution to our understanding of death and dying is the framework of the five stages of grief, introduced in her 1969 book, *On Death and Dying*. Originally called the "5 Stages of Death," and later evolving into variations such as "5 Stages of Grief," "5 Stages of Loss," or simply, the "5 Stages," these stages (denial, anger, bargaining, depression, acceptance) reflect common emotional responses to grief, loss, and change.

- **Denial** is the initial shock and disbelief of loss, intensified when the deceased is young, or their death is sudden and unexpected. The shock of my sister's passing left me in a daze for a long time, unable to grant myself the grace and peace of accepting that she was truly gone.

- **Anger** comes when the unfairness of it all takes center stage. A young mother dies after years battling cancer. Her daughter, Helen, my student, had already passed the stages of shock and denial when she first heard the diagnosis—she had held onto hope that modern medicine would save her mother. When it didn't, Helen was furious. She was angry at the world, at God, at strangers who were outliving her mother despite being decades older. As a hospice intern, she often returned from her shift in tears, shouting at God, demanding to understand why a ninety-five-year-old could thrive while her thirty-nine-year-old mother suffered. At this stage, faith and belief are tested relentlessly.

- **Bargaining** emerges as people try to strike deals—with themselves, with others, but mostly with God. I often hear people say, "I will pray every day, I won't curse, just make my dad get better." Attempt to regain control over the uncontrollable might include: "If I do more charity work, maybe God will let her live. If I study harder and make her happier, she will recover." This stage is illustrated in "Comforting Souls" through little Lauren's bargaining with God about her cat.

- **Depression** sets in when we realize the inevitable that no amount of bargaining, anger, or pleading will change the outcome—it is a dangerous and challenging stage. A sense of hopelessness takes over, and if left unaddressed, this stage can evolve into a more serious depressive state.

- **Acceptance** is the final stage: when we understand that we have no choice but to accept reality. Focus shifts to honoring the wishes of the dying, ensuring their comfort and peace.

These stages were later refined as psychologists recognized that they are interconnected and do not necessarily follow a linear order. Grief does not unfold predictably or in a set order, nor does it have a clear endpoint. The emotional journey can be cyclical, overlapping, and even repetitive as individuals navigate change to accept and adapt to it. One might begin with disbelief and depression, move to bargaining, return to depression, reluctantly accept the reality of loss, only to circle back to anger and despair. Triggers are ever-present, but through grief therapy, we can recognize them and choose how to respond—whether we allow them to consume us or use them to grow.

Perceptions of Death

DOES EVERYONE PERCEIVE death the same way? Certainly not. Age, culture, and gender all shape the way we experience loss and mourning. Older adults tend to approach death with more acceptance than younger generations do. Their attachments and priorities differ vastly and may impact how they grieve. My mother, despite being deeply emotional, viewed death rationally. Having witnessed the loss of friends and relatives, she chose to honor the deceased rather than mourn them.

Given biological differences between men and women, gender also plays a role. Men often grieve pragmatically, finding distractions or immersing themselves in tasks. In my limited observation of our Armenian-American culture, some men create distractions with busy agendas and throw themselves into work while others withdraw entirely, struggling to express their sadness. Many seek escape by self-medicating with alcohol, smoking, or other substances.

In many marriages, the loss of a child is devastating and can lead to separation. It is widely understood that this often happens due to poor communication and a lack of understanding between partners about their different approaches to grieving.

Women's mourning habits can vary based on upbringing and cultural norms. In Anglo-Saxon culture, grief is often private and restrained, with little outward displays of sorrow. Mourning is typically done in solitude, and decorum is always maintained—dramatic displays of emotion like exaggerated crying are uncommon. My British friend Dave lost his brother when he was young, yet he never saw his mother cry. Years later, when Dave asked his mother why she hadn't wept at the funeral or since, she'd simply replied, "I do my mourning in the privacy of my room."

Death and Culture

AMERICAN CULTURE IS a blend of traditions from around the world. Individuals process grief in distinct ways, influenced by their upbringing, beliefs about death, and the social norms and customs of their communities.

Religious traditions play a significant role in burial rites and mourning practices. Christians, Muslims, Jews, Buddhists, and Hindus generally follow customs dictated by their faith.

I am most familiar with Armenian traditions. As the first nation to adopt Christianity, Armenians observe specific rituals when mourning a loss. The night before the funeral, a wake is held where family and friends gather for prayers and quiet reflection with the deceased, followed by refreshments. The funeral itself includes two ceremonies—one in church and one at the gravesite—both led by a priest. Traditional elements such as incense, devotional practices, and liturgical music are incorporated. Mourners adhere to a modest dress code: typically, women wear black with minimal makeup, and men, unshaven, wear suits with black ties.

Following the burial, a meal is shared in honor of the deceased. The mourning period continues for seven days, during which visitors bring food to the family. A memorial service is held on the fortieth day, and for at least five years thereafter, an annual remembrance is observed with prayer services in church, followed by a luncheon. Some Armenians who have adopted evangelical practices follow a simpler Anglo-Saxon approach, with a church service, burial, and luncheon, but without ongoing commemorations.

Muslim funeral rites also emphasize modesty and conclude with communal meals. Historically, some traditions included pagan rituals: wailing, self-mutilation, and head-shaving—practices that have largely disappeared. This aspect is evident in the story of Nadia in "Embracing Loss."

Buddhists, on the other hand, follow an extended mourning process with a series of services held every seven days for seven weeks, sometimes lasting up to a hundred days. They believe it takes this long for the spirit to be fully released. Immediate family members typically wear white, while others may wear black or dark colors. A wake precedes the funeral, and cremation occurs several days after death.

Hindu funerals involve a mourning period of ten to thirty days. Visitors bring food and fruit baskets rather than flowers, and a portrait of the deceased is adorned with garlands of flowers. On the thirteenth day of mourning, a ritual with chants is performed to release the soul for reincarnation. A rice pudding dessert, symbolizing the sweetness of life and the nourishment for the soul, is served.

In Jewish tradition, the initial mourning period, *Aninut*, lasts from the time of death until burial and is especially intense when mourning a parent. Mourners tear their clothing as a sign of sorrow. The seven-day period after the funeral, Shiva, is marked by receiving guests and reciting the Mourner's Kaddish. During Shiva, mourners refrain from personal grooming and intimacy, and cover mirrors as a symbol of introspection.

These traditions display the diverse ways in which humanity copes with loss, offering reassurance to some while evoking anxiety in others. By framing death as a rite of passage, they provide a path toward understanding, and, for many, the hope of reunion with loved ones.

Children's Understanding of Death

As ADULTS, WE understand that death is an inevitable part of life. But how do children comprehend it, and at what age should we introduce them to its complexities?

Children are remarkably resilient. Some display immediate grief when faced with death, while others seem unaffected, making it appear as though they don't care. They process loss in their own way, often expressing sadness at unexpected moments. Patience and reassurance are crucial. It's important to be honest with children—offering simple, age-appropriate answers, or admitting when we don't know, rather than resorting to soothing falsehoods—which is healthier for the child in the long run.

A child's reaction to death varies depending on their maturity and developmental age. Many people view loss in terms of their own needs, asking: "Now that my protector is gone, are my needs going to be met?"

Psychologist Abraham Maslow's Hierarchy of Needs helps explain this response to death. Often depicted as a pyramid (see illustration), it shows the progression of human needs, from the basic physiological requirements to the higher psychological goals. Young children experiencing loss may fear disruptions to their basic needs—Where will I live?" "Who will feed me?" "Will I be okay?"

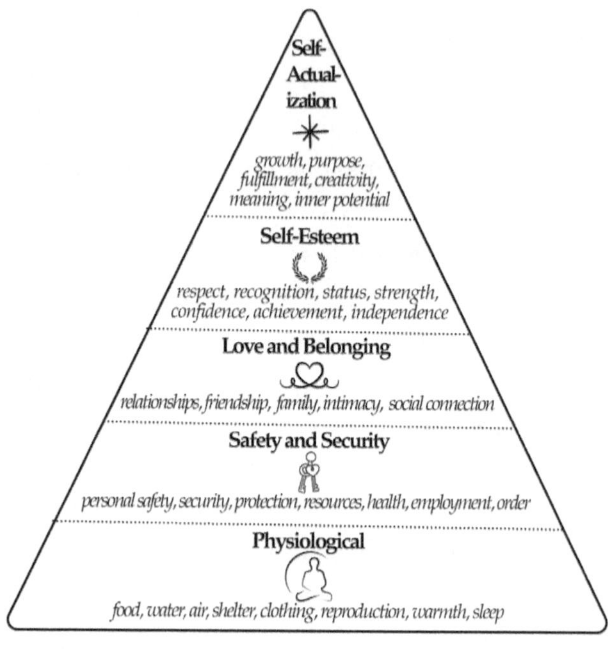

Maslow defines these as *physiological* and *safety* needs. I witnessed this firsthand when my mother suffered a heart attack and was hospitalized for weeks. At the time, I didn't know how to cook and didn't have the time to learn, so she prepared our meals while I managed school and work. One day at the hospital, my five-year-old daughter, teary-eyed and distressed, asked me, "Is Nene going to be okay? When is she coming home? How will we eat?"—a textbook example of Maslow's theory.

For teenagers, grief is often centered on love, belonging, and relationships. The loss of a grandparent, for example, can feel like the loss of family stability.

Adult Relationships with Death

OUR RESPONSE TO loss depends on our relationships and is shaped by those emotional bonds. While the death of an aging parent is expected, it still profoundly affects the surviving child. Losing a parent can feel like losing a part of oneself—especially the inner child who once sought her praise or comfort.

The realization that *I am an orphan now* is common among grieving adults as the inner child realizes that something as simple as giving or receiving a hug from a parent or calling them, saying "Hi, Mom!" is no longer possible.

The absence of a parent's familiar voice, touch, and unconditional love can leave a lasting void. Consequently, when losing a parent, the adult orphan must come to terms with their own mortality and that they, now, may be next in line.

Beyond grief, loss can also affect our self-esteem. The way our parents raised and nurtured us plays a role in our identity and our self-worth, and their absence can force us to reevaluate our place in the world. Some regress emotionally, struggling to accept their new reality. It is essential, however, not to lose our sense of reality and backpedal to childhood.

Coming to terms with death can be a lifelong process. No matter how we rationalize our emotions—whether by suppressing tears, dismissing our feelings, or even overreacting to them—the inner child remains. Feelings of uncertainty, fear, and anger can persist, bringing up a different set of questions at each stage of life. If they become overwhelming or if they are prolonged, seeking professional support is crucial.

Tangible and Intangible Grief

GRIEF ISN'T JUST about losing a person or possession—it extends beyond the tangible. I cannot emphasize the importance of recognizing tangible and intangible grief enough. Tangible grief is straightforward—we mourn the loss of someone or something we can see and touch. But what about intangible grief? The loss of security, identity, or autonomy can be just as devastating, yet often goes unrecognized and unaddressed.

This type of grief can accompany tangible loss. When I moved to the United States as a teenager over fifty years ago, I lost not only my friends and my security but also my entire understanding of the world as I knew it. It wasn't just my room and my bed that was gone—it was my foundation. That loss left me withdrawn, shy, and uncommunicative.

Later in life, leaving a job I had held for twenty years triggered a similar crisis. I lost my autonomy, my stability, and nearly my identity. I felt unmoored, struggling to regain control. Like many adults, I relied on structure and certainty, and when that was taken from me, I fell into a deep emotional fog. I became distrustful of people around me, second-guessing every decision, and questioning every step taken. My anxiety became so overwhelming that I developed short-term aphasia.

Psychotherapist and life coach John Gaspari explores this often-overlooked form of grief extensively in his work, offering valuable insights into how it affects our lives. His blog is a must-read for anyone seeking a deeper understanding of this topic.

Unresolved intangible grief is a silent burden—an unspoken loss that lingers, influencing decisions and creating inner turmoil across one's lifespan. Unlike tangible grief, which is acknowledged and mourned, intangible grief lingers in the background, elusive and insidious. It haunts its bearer, slowly and subtly eroding well-being and a sense of self. Left unaddressed, it becomes a phantom presence—destabilizing, unraveling, and quietly wreaking havoc.

The Last Stages of Life

MUCH IS WRITTEN about the last stages of life, available in books, websites, and blogs—all widely accessible. Yet when I reflect on my journey with grief, I wish someone had prepared me and offered even basic guidance on what to expect.

We must remember that every person's experience is unique. Some decline gradually, like Arti in "Finding Peace," while others pass suddenly, as my mother did in "Guiding Light." The role of caretakers or family members is to ensure that their loved one is comfortable and feels surrounded by love. The following changes often occur in the last stages of a person's life, though not necessarily in this order nor all inclusive:

- Breathing may become irregular, shallow, or include long pauses.
- They may stop eating and drinking.
- Their skin might become pale or appear blotchy.
- They may sleep much more and be difficult to wake.
- They might become restless, anxious, or agitated.
- They may use the bathroom less as their body slows down.
- Their blood pressure and heart rate may drop.
- Their hands, feet, or other parts of their body may feel cold.
- Some might see or talk to people who aren't there, including loved ones who have passed.

These shifts are deeply challenging for caregivers, especially when looking after a loved one. It's essential to take breaks, eat well, and stay hydrated. Witnessing the changes as someone you love nears the end of life is both emotionally and physically exhausting.

Aging and Grief

FOR MOST OF our lives, we are climbing—advancing our careers, earning recognition, building strong bodies, creating homes, and raising children. These pursuits all suggest an upward movement. Aging, however, is the opposite. As we grow older, we retire, often with reduced income and, more significantly, a shift in social status. If once people surrounded us, we may now find ourselves alone.

Our bodies weaken, our memories falter, and we forget simple words or appointments—experiences that can feel disorienting and devastating. Aging often brings loneliness and a sense of emptiness. Many older adults live alone and rarely receive visits from younger family members, intensifying their feelings of isolation and loss. The reality of nearing the end of life becomes undeniable.

Young people, whether consciously or not, tend to overlook the elderly. In my mid-fifties, I found myself juggling too many responsibilities, sometimes forgetting small routines—brushing my hair, applying lipstick. One day, sensing my frustration, a colleague reassured me, "Don't worry, the young don't notice us because we're older, and those older than us can't see much anyway."

We laughed, but her words struck me as both perceptive and true.

Speaking to people in hospice care can reveal common themes: overwhelming sorrow, persistent low mood, emotional distress, and a lingering sadness. Yet mental health can improve dramatically when older adults engage with younger generations in meaningful ways. Activities such as visiting parks and museums, reading and discussing books, or simply sharing stories can help bridge generations and bring joy to both the young and the elderly.

In my practice, I have observed senior programs where overworked social workers lead exercises, followed by meals and presentations—often dominated by the most extroverted participants. While well-intentioned, these efforts often lack the engagement needed to truly uplift the elderly.

In many cultures labeled as "third world," elders are revered, included in daily life, and remain active members of their communities. They engage with both the young and old, often living longer and healthier lives as a result. Inspired by this, I launched an intergenerational program through a nonprofit, pairing high school students with seniors in assisted living facilities. The students spent quality time with the elderly through structured activities, sharing stories, and learning from one another. The seniors, in turn, found joy in storytelling and glimpsing the modern world through young eyes. The students even earned internship hours. Sadly, bureaucratic red tape forced us to discontinue the program.

I still firmly believe that such initiatives benefit both generations—the young gain wisdom and perspective, while the elderly remain mentally engaged and socially connected. Recent research supports this idea: studies of intergenerational programs in nursing homes show that connections between young and old can improve well-being, enhance social inclusion, and reduce ageism. Even the World Health Organization recognizes the importance of intergenerational engagement and has launched its own initiatives to bridge the gap between young and old, aiming for an "age-friendly world."

An African proverb says, "When an elder dies, a library burns to the ground." Only with age do we begin to grasp the true value of the wisdom that came before us.

Social Etiquette in the Face of Death

My earliest memory of embarrassment surrounding death dates to when I was seven, visiting my grandmother in Aleppo, Syria. My Nene's neighbor across the street had just lost her husband suddenly, leaving her a widow after twenty years of marriage. Following Armenian tradition, my mother and Nene prepared food, either delivering it themselves and helping with serving and cleaning or sending it with one of my older siblings.

On that day, none of my siblings were home, so my mother asked me to take a small dish she had just prepared.

She gave me clear instructions: "Make sure you tell her *Kaynke Kezi*"—an Armenian phrase used in times of loss, meaning, "May you inherit the life he was to live."

As an anxious child, I repeated the phrase over and over to myself until I reached the widow's doorstep and rang the bell. When she answered the door, I handed her the dish, and, in my nervousness, I blurted out the wrong phrase: *Darose Kezi*. This expression is said to single people at weddings, and means, "May you be next (to wed)."

The widow, gracious as she was, said nothing. Instead, she gently called my mother to let her know what had happened. Word of my *faux pas* spread through our small community, and the memory of that moment—though now humorous—left a mark on me for life.

What to Say to a Mourner

SOCIAL NORMS DICTATE that we should be polite and sympathetic when offering condolences. Etiquette calls for expressions of compassion to console the mourner, such as:

- *"My condolences for your loss."*
- *"I am so sorry for your loss."*
- *"You and your loved ones are in my thoughts and prayers."*
- *"This is so sad to hear. I'm thinking of you and your family."*

As someone who has heard these sentiments countless times, I have often questioned their meaning. Why are people thinking of us? Are we truly in their thoughts and prayers? Do these phrases offer reassurance? And how are we meant to respond—simply by saying thank you?

I believe there are meaningful ways to offer condolences. For close relationships, it is better to say something more personal, for instance, "I am here for you whenever you need anything." For acquaintances, a simple but heartfelt acknowledgement like, "God rest her soul. She was a good person," feels more sincere.

Never Minimize Someone's Loss

SOMETIMES, WELL-MEANING words can diminish the depth of someone's grief unintentionally. Avoid statements such as:

- *"You have other kids; you must be strong for them."*
- *"That's ok, you'll get another dog."*
- *"It's only a piece of jewelry; you can buy another one."*

Each loss is deeply personal, and a seemingly replaceable object may carry profound meaning and hold sentimental value. I remember a few months after my sister's death, I lost her ring in the school restroom. To this day, I replay that moment with pain, knowing nothing will ever replace that simple single pearl ring.

Be Genuine

AUTHENTICITY IS CRUCIAL when comforting the bereaved. People in grief are emotionally raw and can easily sense when words aren't sincere. Empty platitudes or clichés can feel hollow and dismissive. Most importantly, never tell someone to "get over it already" or suggest that enough time has passed for grief to subside.

After my sister's forty-day memorial service, as I was leaving the church, a distant cousin saw me trying to hold back tears. She approached me and said, "Please stop— you're making me cry."

In that my moment, all I could do was stare at her. I was stunned by her selfishness. I felt anger rise within me, but I simply walked away. I never saw her again.

Unexpected Comfort

AT TIMES, COMFORT comes from the most unexpected of places—a kindred spirit who offers support and eases the pain. Like many Americans, I belong to an HMO, where medical care often feels transactional rather than personal. After my mother passed, I started experiencing physical symptoms brought on by stress and grief. Although I understood the cause, my daughters insisted I see a doctor.

Dr. Patel, a young and intelligent physician, was thorough and knowledgeable. But I never expected her to be so perceptive. When she entered the room, she took one look at me and asked what was wrong. In my fragile state, I kept my explanation brief, careful not to break down. With my head lowered, I braced myself for the usual polite response—a simple "I'm sorry for your loss"—but heard nothing.

When I finally looked up, I saw tears forming in her eyes. Softly, she said she was going through the same thing, having recently lost her father as well.

In that moment, something unspoken passed between us—a quiet understanding of shared grief. For the first time, I allowed myself to fall apart and cry. We didn't exchange stories or offer each other comfort. We simply sat in silence, bound by a shared pain that needed no explanation.

I will never forget what she did for me during my most vulnerable time.

Ernest Hemingway once said, "In our darkest moments, we don't need solutions or advice; we yearn for simple human connection, a quiet presence, gentle touch. These small gestures are the anchors that hold us steady when life feels like too much."

Grief is not something to be fixed—it is something to be carried. As you navigate your own loss and work through your inner storms, don't seek quick solutions. Instead, reach out to a steady hand—a loved one, a friend, or even a stranger—someone who can simply sit with you in your sorrow and, perhaps, guide you along your path.

War and Grief

Dedicated to all who have witnessed the devastations of war and the generations of survivors who preserve their legacies through personal and collective memories.

I WOULD BE remiss not to address war and grief, having witnessed conflict firsthand and carried the collective trauma of my ancestors, beginning with the 1915 Armenian Genocide—the first documented genocide—in which my great-grandparents perished. Our personal losses are often deepened by the traumatic memories passed down from our ancestors. These haunting legacies persist beyond their suffering to shape us. In many ways, these themes—war, grief, memory—run through several of the stories in this book. Unfortunately, humanity has not learned from its past mistakes. To this day, in the twenty-first century, we continue to witness atrocities that humans inflict upon one another.

I grew up during wartime in Damascus, Syria, where my family lived. My grandmother's stories of her mother's death during the Armenian Genocide, on April 14, 1915, were shared with us every year. These stories not only reminded us of our past but also emphasized the importance of preserving our identity, language, and religion. We held vigils at church to remember and honor our loved ones, and I was taught in detail about the atrocities committed by the Ottoman Empire. My grandmother's words resonated with me then and still do today. This was the struggle I lived with before I witnessed the war in Syria.

In 1973, Egypt and Syria went to war against Israel in what we called the Golan War and what was known elsewhere as the Yom Kippur War or October War. Israel bombed the city of Damascus, striking the area where foreign embassies were located, two blocks from our home. I remember the day my father informed us of the ongoing conflict and the likelihood that Damascus would be targeted. He explained what we should do, though, in truth, there wasn't much we could do.

We lived on the second floor of a three-story building and were advised to move to the third floor in case the building collapsed, so we wouldn't be buried under rubble. I overheard my father telling my mother that given our proximity to potential bombing targets, our chances of survival were dismal. Fear and frustration mounted within us as we found ourselves at the epicenter of a conflict that had nothing to do with us—we were neither Arab, Muslim, nor Jew.

Syria, a historically Muslim country, had long been a haven for many, including my great-grandparents, Christian-Armenians who had fled the genocide seeking refuge. My maternal and paternal great-grandparents were medical school graduates and had built a life for their children, never anticipating another war. Now, more than fifty years after our ancestral genocide, we were facing a foreign war. The atmosphere in our home was filled with panic, anxiety, and apprehension.

There was no time to think, plan, or flee. I remember the first bomb. I was on the balcony, looking at the empty street below. Once bustling with people and merchants, it was now eerily silent. I heard a faint hiss, then a noise like the whistling of fireworks just before they explode. Then came a loud crash, followed by a shockwave that rattled the building. I ran inside, covering my head from flying glass and debris. My mother urged us to stay with her, fear in her eyes. We gathered in the sitting room, waiting, listening, anticipating the worst. Another muffled explosion sounded, seemingly farther away.

The electricity went out, and communication with the outside world ceased. Thankfully, my mother had already stored food, candles, and blankets to carry us through a few days.

The attacks on Damascus lasted almost a week. When the bombing stopped, people poured out of their homes, walking through the streets, searching for damage, and sharing stories of fear, panic, and deprivation. My friends and I headed toward the embassies to see the aftermath: buildings had collapsed into unstable rubble. The destruction—piles and piles of debris, twisted metal, and shattered glass—barely conveyed our deep insecurity. Policemen yelled at children to stay away, but no one moved.

We were stunned, unable to look away from the devastation. My father caught up and scolded us, warning never to return to that place again. My mind went numb. I couldn't think of anything else. For nights afterward, I relived the bombing. The same explosions I'd heard from the balcony haunted me in nightmares, jolting me awake.

The next few months were filled with funerals, mourners expressing their grief in different ways. At home, we moved through our days in a daze—barely speaking, barely functioning. The shock of what happened left us in a mental stupor, unable to grasp its full scale and impact. It was then and there that my mother decided it was time for us to leave Syria and move to the United States, where her family lived and where we would be safe.

My mother sent my older sister first to pursue her studies. The following year, she sold everything and moved us to the United States, carrying with her a veil of grief and uncertainty.

It is undeniable that our ancestral war, the Armenian Genocide, left our identity intact but displaced. My great-grandparents lost not only their homes but also the hope and meaning that displacement brings. In turn, we lost our autonomy.

As we tried to plant our roots and establish ourselves as Americans, we faced significant resistance, despite entering the country legally. My mother struggled to feel safe, her sense of security forever unsettled, always bracing for the next disaster. She planned our futures but never allowed herself to imagine her own. Whenever she reflected on her life, her thoughts were clouded by loss.

As children, we struggled to define our identities— displaced Armenians born in Syria, a foreign land that did not reflect our beliefs. Then we moved again, navigating a new language, new customs, and the silent expectations of assimilation. But full acceptance demanded a price we were unwilling, yet pressured, to pay.

I quickly realized that to fit in, I had to lose my accent. I spent hours taking lessons, reshaping my speech. If I spoke without an accent, I reasoned, I would finally belong, escape ridicule, and perhaps, find my own individuality and freedom.

Still, grief weighed on me. Most of the time, I was a stranger to myself, burdened by the grief I carried. I tried to reinvent myself, only to realize I was avoiding the inevitable—acknowledging and embracing that grief. Though therapy and self-analysis helped, I recently experienced one of the most intense emotional outbursts I'd had in years.

My friend and colleague, Dr. Lupe Zuniga, and I went to see *Oppenheimer*. Toward the end of the movie, as the first atomic bomb detonated, the theater fell silent. Lupe, knowing my history, turned to me and whispered, "A delayed sound effect is coming." Then I heard it—the same sound that had shaken our home in Damascus. Instinctively, I covered my head, just as I had in 1973. My heart pounded for fifteen minutes while Lupe tried to calm me with breathing exercises and quiet reassurance.

I hadn't expected to react that way. I knew that the movie contained scenes of bombings and explosions—after all, I had read the reviews. And yet, for two weeks afterward, the war I had witnessed returned in my dreams, forcing me to confront just how much I'd suppressed. My grief had hardened into something unspoken, something that had shaped me in ways I was only beginning to understand.

Grief, I've come to realize, is a form of self-preservation. There is no ideal way to express it—grief takes on different forms for each of us, influenced by our values, upbringing, and culture. Healing doesn't come with time alone; recovery depends on whether we allow ourselves to process that grief—with or without help, through therapy or something else.

Memories serve as a profound testament to how we have lived our lives, rich with deep, lasting connections that form our identities. Each recollection is a private treasure, sacred in its significance, reminding us of the experiences that have molded our perspectives.

Next time you find yourself lost in memory—whether remembering a loved one or retracing the past—and feel that familiar ache rising, take a moment to reflect. Those memories are not mere remnants of the past, but the very foundations upon which you build your future. Embrace the love shared. Wrap yourself in a blanket, close your eyes, and let the moment unfold. Allow the feeling to move through you slowly and settle. Relish the incredible relationships you have cultivated. If tears come, smile, and acknowledge the beauty of your vulnerability and strength, for they are the essence of a life well-lived.

Epilogue

⟿∽⟿

Los Angeles, January 2025

JUST AS I reached the final pages of this book, the fires erupted. They ignited simultaneously across Los Angeles—raging through Altadena and Pasadena, engulfing Eaton Canyon, tearing through Pacific Palisades, consuming Malibu, and creeping into Sherman Oaks and Encino.

Growing up in California, I learned to live with its wild temper—earthquakes and fires are part of its identity, and mine. But no matter how familiar we become with natural disasters and surviving them, the sight of their aftermath inevitably reshapes our perspective on life.

That afternoon, I glanced up from my desk, expecting to admire the quiet beauty of my garden outside, only to find the sky transformed. The familiar Los Angeles blue fractured, overtaken by a chaotic swirl of shifting colors—fiery orange, blood-red, and a sickly, unsettling gold. I stepped closer. Flames stretched skyward, furious and mesmerizing; their embers carried on the wind like vicious spirits.

Fire—the most beautiful and most ruinous of elements—was devouring everything in its infernal path.

By nightfall, the winds picked up, and the fire responded in kind, spreading with terrifying precision towards the mountains looming over our city. The first responders fought back with equal determination, battling the blaze with unwavering resolve.

For my family, the fight was personal. My son-in-law, Adam, was one of those brave firefighters on the front lines. Each time disaster struck, our fears multiplied—concern for our home, sorrow for our city, and dread for the loss of our pasts. But above all, we feared for the lives of those risking everything to stop the destruction.

Then, without warning, came the call to evacuate.

I had prepared a "just-in-case" bag—a small, futile attempt at grasping control in an uncontrollable situation. Yet when it came time to leave, I hesitated.

All my life, fire had been my greatest fear. I imagined panicking when faced with it—but instead, a strange calm settled over me. What do you decide to take when everything is at risk? Which picture, which book, which memento carries the weight of your life? That choice was taken from me when the firefighters knocked at our door.

"Go," they said. "Now."

We gathered our essentials—our bag, our pets—and walked away. Before stepping into the car, I turned for one last look at our home. I thought of my mother—how she had loved and nurtured this house, cradling generations of memories. It had even endured a powerful earthquake without a crack, as if blessed. "God is protecting me," she had said then, and I found myself whispering those same words now. I silently prayed that the firefighters would hold the line—that we'd have something to return to. And then my thoughts turned to Adam, to all the men and women standing between the flames and our futures, and I prayed for them too.

We were among the fortunate. The fire was contained just two blocks from our home. When we returned, the air was thick with smoke, the ground littered with ash, but our house still stood. Others were not as lucky. In Pacific Palisades and Altadena, entire neighborhoods were reduced to skeletal remains. Streets that had once been filled with life were now wastelands of charred ruins. News outlets called it apocalyptic. Among the destruction, some homes remained untouched, spared by some inexplicable twist of fate. Perhaps, they, too, were blessed.

How much of this destruction was our doing as humans? We push against nature, exploiting its gifts and turning a blind eye to the consequences—until it finally pushes back, with relentless force. We mistake power for wisdom, profit for progress, while the earth keeps score.

And yet, among the wreckage, another truth revealed itself. Neighbors helped neighbors. Strangers offered shelter, food, and comfort. First responders who had lost their own homes continued to fight for others. In the heart of devastation, resilience flourished.

Whether from natural disasters or man-made wars, I knew what it meant to lose a home—not just physically, but in the way it becomes part of your soul, determining both who you are and what you grieve for a lifetime. I also knew what it takes to rebuild again—it can be done, from the ground up, and while it may demand everything you have, it's possible.

The wheel of fortune had turned, and for once, I wasn't caught beneath it. This time, I stood above it, with gratitude—humbled but unbroken. Even in loss, there is survival; even in ruin, there is rebirth. In that moment, I understood what it meant to stand in the path of destruction, to fight against forces greater than yourself, to feel the weight of loss and keep moving forward.

The fires took much. But they didn't take everything. And in what remains, we begin again.

I've told my children that when I die, to release balloons in the sky to celebrate that I graduated. For me, death is a graduation.

—Dr. Elisabeth Kübler-Ross

May the road rise up to greet you
May the wind be always at your back
May the sunshine warm your faces
The rain soft upon your fields
And until we meet again
May God hold you in the palm of his hand

—A Traditional Irish Blessing

Verch
(The End)

Acknowledgements

THE ADAGE "it takes a village" underscores the fundamental truth of communal support in nurturing individuals. As I navigate life's challenges, I do so because of the presence of my supportive village. These amazing individuals—whether family or friends—have provided invaluable guidance and encouragement. They have enriched my experiences and reinforced my belief that I can accomplish my dream. Their support not only nurtured my creativity but also strengthened my trust in this being the right path to take.

My gratitude goes to my beautiful daughters: Sonia, whose gentle and empathic push fostered personal growth, and Niki, whose trust in my abilities and unwavering love encouraged me to start writing. Niki, I could not have done this without our brainstorming—your incredible ideas shaped both the beginning and the ending of this book.

To my husband, whose unrelenting silent looks of encouragement urged me to do what I must, and my sister Jules—the chairwoman of my "booster club"—who tirelessly read every chapter, cheered me on, and double-checked the accuracy of events, I thank you.

To Aza, my beautiful niece, whose kind words and positive feedback lifted my spirits and helped me persevere. To my amazing editor and niece Sona—your work is phenomenal! You seem to navigate my thoughts and ideas as if from within my head. I could not have finished this without you.

To Aline, Alexandra, Ara, and Adam, thank you for your love and for being part of my village.

And finally, thank you to all who took the time to read this book. You have breathed life into the words I have written, and I am profoundly grateful for your care and attention in honoring the people whose stories I have shared.

Notes

Unless otherwise noted, epigraphs are quoted from *The Kübler-Ross Foundation* website, https://www.ekr foundation.org/elisabeth-kubler-ross/quotes/.

All websites were last accessed on March 9, 2025.

ABOUT GRIEF, BEREAVEMENT, AND MOURNING

1. ***The anguish experienced after significant loss … sorrow for a mishap to oneself***–American Psychological Association. s.v. "grief." *APA Dictionary of Psychology*. https://dictionary.apa.org/grief.

2. ***I hope the grief stays with me***–Anderson Cooper, host, *All There Is*, podcast, season 3, episode: "Andrew Garfield's Grief," produced by Anderson Cooper, CNN, September 2, 2022, https://www.cnn.com/audio/podcasts/all-there-is-with-anderson-cooper.

3. ***If you are grateful for your life***–Anderson Cooper, host, *All There Is*, podcast, season 1, episode: "Stephen Colbert: Grateful for Grief," produced by Anderson Cooper, CNN, September 2, 2022, https://www.cnn.com/audio/podcasts/all-there-is-with-anderson-cooper.

ON DEATH AND DYING

4. ***We need to teach the next generation***–Elisabeth Kübler-Ross, quoted from *The Elisabeth Kübler-Ross Foundation* website, https://www.ekrfoundation.org/elisabeth-kubler-ross/quotes/.

5. ***The "5 Stages of Death"***–See Elisabeth Kübler-Ross, *On Death and Dying* (New York: Macmillan, 1969). For more on the evolution of these stages see also, *The Elisabeth Kübler-Ross Foundation* website, https://www.ekrfoundation.org/5-stages-of-grief/5-stages-grief/.

6. ***Grief does not unfold predictably***–For more information on the grief journey, see Elisabeth Kübler-Ross, *Questions and Answers on Death and Dying* (New York: Macmillan, 1974). The "5 Stages" have since been adapted into the "Kübler-Ross Change Curve®," see *The Elisabeth Kübler-Ross Foundation* website, https://www.ekrfoundation.org/5-stages-of-grief/change-curve/.

7. ***Death and culture***–Certified grief counselor Dr. Alejandra Vasquez describes grieving rituals across various cultures and religions in "How Different Cultures Deal with Grief," *Cake*, https://www.joincake.com/blog/how-different-cultures-deal-with-grief/. For an overview of Jewish mourning practices, see also "Burial and Mourning," *My Jewish Learning* website, https://www.myjewishlearning.com/article/burial-and-mourning/.

8. ***Maslow's "Hierarchy of Needs"***–The illustration of Maslow's "Hierarchy of Needs" is an original, minimalist representation created specifically for this book by the author. Abraham Maslow introduced his Hierarchy of Needs framework in his seminal work, "A Theory of Human Motivation," *Psychological Review* 50, no. 4 (1943): 370-396, outlining fundamental human needs from the physiological to self-actualization. He later expanded this framework in *Motivation and Personality* (New York: Harper & Row, 1954). For a simplified overview, see also Saul McLeod, PhD, "Maslow's Hierarchy of Needs," *Simply Psychology* website, https://www.simplypsychology.org/maslow.html.

9. ***Categories and types of grief***–For more on grief, its symptoms, and types, see the *Cleveland Clinic* website, "Grief," https://my.clevelandclinic.org/health/diseases/24787-grief.

10. ***Tangible and intangible grief or loss***–John Gaspari's blog, *Psychotherapy & Coaching Across the Life Span* (https://www.johngaspari.com/) covers a variety of topics related to grief and loss, including "Tangible and Intangible Loss," https://www.johngaspari.com/post/tangible-vs-intangible-loss.

THE LAST STAGES OF LIFE

11. ***End-of-life changes and the stages of dying***–Various online medical sources are available including "Journey's End: Active Dying," on *WebMD*, https://www.webmd.com/palliative-care/journeys-end-active-dying. For insights from end-of-life practitioners with direct experience, see Katie Duncan, *The Dying Process: Your Essential Guide to Understanding Signs, Symptoms & Changes at the End of Life* (Leeds: Singing Dragon, 2019) and Julie McFadden RN, *Nothing to Fear: Demystifying Death to Live More Fully* (New York: Hay House, 2024). McFadden also shares tips as Hospice Nurse Julie, @ hospicenursejulie on TikTok, https://www.tiktok.com/discover/hospice-nurse-julie. For a spiritual perspective, see Trudy Harris, "A Hospice Nurse Finds Glimpses of Heaven in Caregiving," *Guideposts*, https://guideposts.org/positive-living/health-and-wellness/caregiving/hope-and-inspiration/stories-of-hope-for-caregivers/a-hospice-nurse-finds-glimpses-of-heaven-in-caregiving/.

12. ***Aging and fulfillment***–For more on finding fulfillment while aging, see Frank Tallis, *The Act of Living: What the Great Psychologists Can Teach Us About Finding Fulfillment* (New York: Basic Books, 2020).

13. ***Intergenerational programs in nursing homes***–See Bernadette Laging et al., "The Delivery of Intergenerational Programmes in the Nursing Home Setting and Impact on Adolescents and Older Adults: A Mixed Studies Systematic Review." *International Journal of Nursing Studies* 133 (September 2022): 104281, https://doi.org/10.1016/j.ijnurstu.2022.104281.

14. ***"Age-friendly world"***–See "Intergenerational Solidarity and Adolescent Wellbeing," *World Health Organization (WHO)*, https://www.who.int/news/item/12-08-2022-intergenerational-solidarity-and-adolescent-wellbeing.

15. ***Ernest Hemingway once said, "In our darkest moments"***–Commonly attributed to Ernest Hemingway in secondary sources on the web, including social media and blogs, circa late 2024. No primary source in Hemingway's published works or correspondence has been confirmed as of March 9, 2025.

WAR AND GRIEF

16. ***Passage of traumatic memories through the generations***–For more on how traumatic experiences are passed

down through generations and the phenomenon of "postmemory," described by literary scholar Marianne Hirsch, see "The Generation of Postmemory," *Poetics Today* 29, no. 1 (Spring 2008): 103, https://doi.org/10.1215/03335372-2007-019.

Further Reading

Duncan, Katie. *The Dying Process: Your Essential Guide to Understanding Signs, Symptoms & Changes at the End of Life*. Leeds: Singing Dragon, 2019.

Elisabeth Kübler-Ross Foundation. "5 Stages of Grief." Accessed March 9, 2025. https://www.ekrfoundation. org/5-stages-of-grief/5-stages-grief/.

Kübler-Ross, Elisabeth, ed. *Death: The Final Stage of Growth*. Englewood Cliffs, NJ: Prentice-Hall, 1975.

Kübler-Ross, Elisabeth. *On Death and Dying*. New York: Macmillan, 1969.

Kübler-Ross, Elisabeth. *Questions and Answers on Death and Dying*. New York: Macmillan, 1974.

Kübler-Ross, Elisabeth. *The Wheel of Life: A Memoir of Living and Dying*. New York: Scribner, 1997.

Maslow, Abraham H. "A Theory of Human Motivation." *Psychological Review* 50, no. 4 (1943): 370-396.

Maslow, Abraham H. *Motivation and Personality*. New York: Harper & Row, 1954.

McFadden, Julie, RN. *Nothing to Fear: Demystifying Death to Live More Fully*. New York: Hay House, 2024.

McLeod, Saul. "Maslow's Hierarchy of Needs." *Simply Psychology*. Accessed March 9, 2025. https://www.sim-plypsychology.org/maslow.html.

Tallis, Frank. *The Act of Living: What the Great Psychologists Can Teach Us About Finding Fulfillment*. New York: Basic Books, 2020.

About the Author

DR. MARAL YERANOSSIAN holds a doctorate in psychology and applies an eclectic range of methods and approaches in her work with diverse populations. She draws on years of experience to offer insight and compassion, helping others navigate loss through her writing. She lives in California with her family. This is her first book.